Kingdom Authority
on Earth

Bringing Heaven to Your House

Kingdom Authority on Earth
Bringing Heaven to Your House

ISBN-13: 978-0692229019 (Anointed Fire)
ISBN-10: 0692229019

Disclaimer: This book is designed to provide information and motivation to our readers. It is sold with the understanding that the publisher is not engaged to render any type of psychological, legal, or any other kind of professional advice. No warranties or guarantees are expressed or implied by the author, since every man has his own measure of faith. The individual author(s) shall not be liable for any physical, psychological, emotional, financial, or commercial damages, including; but not limited to, special, incidental, consequential or other damages. Our views and rights are the same: You are responsible for your own choices, actions, and results.

The stories in this book are fictional. Names, characters, businesses, places, events and incidents are either the products of the author's imagination or used in a fictitious manner. Any resemblance to actual persons, living or dead, or actual events is purely coincidental.

Acknowledgments

I can only give thanks to GOD, for HE is the Author and Creator of me, and the wisdom found in this book.

Table of Contents

Introduction

There are many laws governing the spirit realm that most believers are unaware of. We read the Bible, and with so many words jumping off the pages at us, we often find ourselves grabbing onto whatever we can understand and putting away the rest for later. Needless to say, we have to understand the entire WORD of GOD to better understand life as a whole. After all, the Bible is our instruction guide to living, and our road map to Heaven. Our lives won't change until our minds change, and our minds won't change until they've been bathed in wisdom, clothed with knowledge and perfumed with understanding.

There are laws governing marriage, relationships, wealth, poverty, and everything that exists in the realm of the earth. But when we are unaware of these laws, we can't enjoy the benefits of being law-abiding citizens for the Kingdom of GOD. Instead, we often find ourselves on the other side of a stronghold, not understanding what we did to get there.

Kingdom Authority on Earth: Bringing Heaven to Your House is a wisdom-packed guide to helping you better understand how to finally tap into the blessings of GOD, without tripping over the strongholds that have enslaved and robbed so many believers today. Learn how to finally take back what GOD has given you, and to uproot whatever the enemy has planted in your hearts.

Kingdom Authority: Bringing Heaven to Your House will teach you:

- How to bring Heaven to your house
- How to tap into Kingdom wealth
- The laws about relationships
- How to receive what you've been praying for
- And much more

The wait is over. All you need to do is understand what CHRIST JESUS did for you and how to tap into the blessings of GOD, and the WORD will do the rest.

Kingdom Authority

Every kingdom has laws, and every kingdom has law enforcement. Without laws, a kingdom would be overtaken by evil, and there would be no consequences for evil.

When Adam and Eve were created, there was only one law, and that was: They were never to eat from the Tree of the Knowledge of Good and Evil. This law was designed by GOD to protect them since evil was in the world. If they hadn't bit of the fruit, they would have remained innocent and without blemish. In other words, they would have been perfect and GOD would have continued to provide for them. But they disobeyed GOD and bit the fruit, and now ... the rest is history.

Nowadays, the earth is full of sin and sinners. The earth is polluted by evil; nevertheless, GOD has remained the same. HE still loves us enough to protect us from the evil therein, but because HE made us in HIS image, we can use our built in will to decide what choices we want to make. Unfortunately, because of the sinful nature of our flesh, our choices often mirror the choices of Adam and Eve, thus causing us to be evicted from our paradises and sent into our wildernesses where we find ourselves lost, hungry and afraid. Let's face it: GOD loves us and HE has wonderful plans for us, but we've got to learn to trust HIM.

Jeremiah 29:11-13: *For I know the thoughts that I think toward you, saith the LORD, thoughts of peace, and not of evil, to give you an expected end. Then shall ye call upon me, and ye shall go and pray unto me, and I will hearken unto you. And ye shall seek me, and find me, when ye shall search for me with all your heart.*

John 10:10: *The thief cometh not, but for to steal, and to kill, and to destroy: I am come that they might have life, and that they might* *have it more abundantly.*

Despite all of our flaws, GOD still loves us, and HE is still very protective of us. For this reason, HE sent HIS only begotten SON to die for us. Before CHRIST came into the realm of the earth, mankind was not justified by the law; he was condemned by it. The law was made to reprove a man, but it could not justify him. The law condemned the sinner, but CHRIST condemned the sin and justified the sinner. To justify means to make righteous or declare just. **Romans 8:1:** *There is therefore now no condemnation to them which are in Christ Jesus, who walk not after the flesh, but after the Spirit.*

Most people are waiting to go to Heaven, but the LORD wants us to learn to enjoy Heaven right here on Earth. HE wants us to learn to tap into Heaven and pull down the blessings thereof. Howbeit, we are visual creatures who tend to minimize the blessings we see everyday in order to maximize what's wrong in our lives. We can wake up (blessing), enjoy a hot meal (blessing), go to work (blessing), earn a decent day's salary (blessing), arrive home safely to our families (blessing), and still call the day a bad day if we had a flat tire and a cranky boss. Why is this? The enemy is still up to his old tricks. Adam and Eve were surrounded by paradise and lived in the very presence of GOD; nevertheless, they were still able to focus on a little fruit hanging off a tree branch. They still desired what they could not have, and they allowed the enemy to blind them to the fact that they were blessed. The enemy knew that mankind had will; he therefore tempted Eve to act upon her will in the wrong way. We're still the same today. We're blessed of GOD, but we oftentimes only tend to see what's wrong or what we cannot have rather than focusing on all that's right and what we do have.

Now that CHRIST has died for our sins, and given us access to Heavenly things, we can reach up to Heaven (in faith) and pull down the blessings of GOD, but most people don't know this. Many of us were taught to religiously and ritually go to church, read our Bibles (but not comprehend the WORD), and follow a set of Biblical rules; howbeit, not too many people were actually taught to worship and love the LORD. Because of this, many children who were brought up in church denounce their faith when they get older. The issue isn't that they don't love the LORD; the problem is they don't know the LORD, they know religion, and we all know that religion can be hideous, repulsive and full of judgmental, self-righteous sinners with an appetite for blood. Trying to win them for the actual Kingdom of GOD is oftentimes difficult because people have learned to link religion with GOD, and we have to be honest with ourselves: If we didn't know GOD, but we only knew religion, most of us would run away from the church as well. Religion is ritualistic, judgmental, law-filled and almost impossible to live in; nevertheless, true holiness is a lifestyle that is brought on by our love of GOD and a changed mind. Holiness is beautiful and most people who experience it love the freedom that comes with it.

GOD has already declared the blessings that would overtake the righteous, and the punishments that would come upon the unrighteous. Because the WORD will not return to GOD void, every word HE has spoken has been established; therefore, any choices we make determine whether we'll invoke a blessing or a chastening. We are Kingdom citizens, so when we are Kingdom-minded, we get to enjoy the fruits of the Kingdom of GOD. When we rebel against the WORD, we shackle ourselves to the law of the flesh, and the law represents condemnation, fear and bondage.

What can we do to invoke the blessings of GOD to overtake us? It's simple. We must walk in the will of GOD to enjoy the will of GOD. What does this mean? It is the will of

GOD that we be healthy. It is the will of GOD
that we be wealthy. It is the will of GOD that
we have a sound mind (peace). Nevertheless, it
is also the will of GOD that we walk in love
towards one another. It is also the will of GOD
that we not fornicate, commit adultery, lie,
steal, gossip, backbite, revel or commit any sins
that go against the New Testament law of love.
So in order for us to enjoy good health,
abundance, peace and all that GOD has for us,
we must first learn to love GOD with all of our
hearts, souls and strength. When we love HIM,
we will honor HIM. When we love ourselves or
our flesh more than we love HIM, we lose sight
of HIM as we begin to focus on ourselves.

So what should we do to bring the Kingdom of
Heaven into the realm of the earth? We bring
Heaven into our hearts by bringing the WORD
into our hearts to live there. We evict all that is
not of GOD, and when Heaven lives on the
inside of us, we can speak Heavenly things into
the earth realm. When we have the WORD of

GOD in us, we can change the atmosphere wherever we go. We can tear down powers and principalities and establish Kingdom authority wherever we live. Alone, we can recruit citizens for the Kingdom of GOD because, when someone sees Heaven's light shining from within us, they will automatically be drawn to that light. The problem is there are more religious people out there than there are people who actually know the WORD and live it.

First, we must learn to identify who we are and what we have. For example, what do you see when you look in the mirror? Most people would say that they see themselves; howbeit, what you see in the mirror is not actually "you", it's your flesh. You are a spirit who lives in a flesh suit; therefore, you cannot see yourself. You can only see your covering. So, we must learn to understand just what our bodies are. Our bodies are the temple of the HOLY SPIRIT. When we stop calling our bodies "our bodies" and begin to call them "our temples", we'll respect and care for them better. We'll stop feeding them foods that are designed to fill them up but not nurture them; foods that are linked to high blood pressure, diabetes and obesity. When we learn to identify our bodies as temples, we'll stop submitting our bodies to fornication (a sin offering to the devil) and start submitting our bodies as living sacrifices, holy and acceptable to GOD, for this is our reasonable service (*see Romans 12:1*).

Next, we have to learn to identify our souls (mind, will and emotions), and understand how they link to our hearts. Our hearts are like our engines. They are the command centers of our souls, and our souls are directly linked to our hearts. Whatever gets past our imaginations eventually gets into our hearts, and becomes a heart condition. If the WORD of GOD gets into our hearts, the WORD will begin to flow from us, and we are identified as ministers of the gospel (good news/ truth). If lies get into our hearts, lies will begin to flow from us, thus causing us to be identified as liars.

Whatever we allow into our hearts, we allow behind the wheels of our lives.

Additionally, we must know and understand what a stronghold is. A stronghold is an imprisonment of our souls. It can be demonic imprisonment through bad habits, generational mindsets and wrongful beliefs, or it can simply be the manifestation of a lack of knowledge. A stronghold is whatever belief that's strong enough to hold our minds in captivity.

Finally, we need to understand what our flesh is. Our flesh isn't just our bodies; our flesh is the systems of our bodies. We all have a system that we've grown accustomed to, and many of these systems have been developed through strongholds. For example, if our parents lived in poverty and never attempted to break out of poverty (which, of course, is a mindset), we are more likely to live in and remain in poverty. Only a small percentage of children growing up in poverty actually escape these conditions and mindsets.

Most people have the same systems:

- Wake up in the morning.
- Take a shower.
- Get dressed for work.
- Grab a cup of coffee on the way out of the door.
- Go to work.
- Dread the job.
- Come home.
- Cook.
- Help the children with their homework.
- Take a shower.
- Go to bed.

If you attempt to introduce a different system to someone who's comfortable with their flesh's system, you are likely to be met with resistance. The truth is: Most people want more, but only few are willing to step out and grab more.

Our flesh is also linked to our beliefs. Wrongful beliefs don't deposit themselves in our spirit man; they go directly to the flesh. Lies and false doctrines cannot root themselves in our eternal being (spirits) because our spirits are holy through CHRIST JESUS. Lies and false doctrines root themselves in our flesh (external systems) and not our spirit.

Galatians 5:16-24: *This I say then, Walk in the Spirit, and ye shall not fulfil the lust of the flesh. For the flesh lusteth against the Spirit, and the Spirit against the flesh: and these are contrary the one to the other: so that ye cannot do the things that ye would. But if ye be led of the Spirit, ye are not under the law. Now the works of the flesh are manifest, which are these; Adultery, fornication, uncleanness, lasciviousness, idolatry, witchcraft, hatred, variance, emulations, wrath, strife, seditions, heresies, envyings, murders, drunkenness, revellings, and such like: of the which I tell you before, as I have also told you in time past, that they which do such things shall not inherit the* *kingdom of God. But the fruit of the Spirit is love, joy, peace, longsuffering, gentleness, goodness, faith, meekness, temperance: against such there is no law. And they that are Christ's have crucified the flesh with the affections and lusts.*

Again, our flesh is our systems. One good way to identify your system is to write down your day-to-day activities for twenty-one days. Why twenty-one days? Because it takes seventeen to twenty-one days to break a habit. A habit is a self-imposed tradition that we perform out of familiarity. Once you've identified your system, try breaking all that's wrong with it. You'll notice that you can steer away from your flesh's system for about seven days without fail, but after seven days, the flesh begins to rebel, and this is when we are oftentimes pulled back into our systems. Our flesh doesn't mind us taking a vacation from its rituals, but it begins to violently and loudly oppose us when we attempt to break up with our systems.

After we've learned to identify who we are, what we are and our purposes in life, it's easier for us to make lifestyle adjustments and invite Heaven into our hearts.

Kingdom authority is the authority given to us on Earth, as it is in Heaven through CHRIST JESUS. Kingdom authority is our ability to walk in the confidence and authority of GOD. It is our ability to cause our worlds (realities) to mirror Heaven by simply changing our minds and speaking the WORD of GOD in faith. It is our ability to move mountains, walk on water, tread upon serpents, heal the sick, raise the dead and do everything that CHRIST was able to do.

Luke 10:19: *Behold, I give unto you power to tread on serpents and scorpions, and over all the power of the enemy: and nothing shall by any means hurt you.*

To walk in Kingdom authority, we must learn to speak the language of the Kingdom of GOD, and know the will of GOD for our lives. If we don't know the will of GOD, it'll be harder for us to access the blessings of GOD, because the enemy is not shy in telling us what his will is for us. To walk in Kingdom authority, we must:

1. Know the WORD of GOD (knowledge). When we have knowledge of who GOD is, we learn to acknowledge HIM as GOD.
2. Understand the WORD of GOD (understanding). When we understand the WORD, we stand on the WORD.
3. Search the heart of understanding for the depth of GOD'S WORD (wisdom). When we go into the depths of wisdom, we learn Kingdom authority, for it is much more than what meets the eye.

Of course, with wisdom, knowledge and understanding, we learn to fear and love the LORD. When we fear HIM, we learn to reverence the LORD and acknowledge HIS power. When we love HIM, we learn to favor

GOD over ourselves, and it is easier for us to do HIS will, since we naturally want to please whomever we love.

Faith gives us access to Kingdom authority, but fear grants Satan access to us. Walk in the confidence of the WORD of GOD, and the enemy will hear and fear your every footstep. There are many laws that will help us to bring Heaven home with us, and we must know and understand these laws before we can reap the benefits thereof.

The Law of Transfer

Have you ever had one of those days when you were in a great mood? On that particular day, you were overjoyed about something or someone, and you were excited about what the rest of the day would bring. But suddenly, that family member, friend or foe came to you in a bad mood. Something happened to them that day that upset them, and they couldn't wait to transfer that negative energy to you. Before you knew it, they were either yelling at you or yelling to you, and just like that, your joy did what you should have done: It got up and left. After that, you were even more upset than they were, but for some strange reason, they seemed to feel a lot better. If they were complaining to you as a friend, they may have even told you that they felt better, and thanked you as you carried that load with you while

they ran off with your peace of mind. What
happened in that moment? Someone gave to
you what they should have given to the LORD,
but you are not and were not equipped to hold
it.

Psalm 55:22: *Cast thy burden upon the LORD,
and he shall sustain thee: he shall never suffer
the righteous to be moved.*

You were moved because you were not created
to carry negative energy. The human race as a
whole or individually cannot carry negativity.
The load is too heavy for us. But should we
reject a friend when they need a shoulder to
cry on? Of course not. Well, not unless they
are always crying and complaining about
something or someone. In that case, you'd
have to refer them to the LORD because the
issue isn't rooted in the situations; the issue is
what's in their heart. The situations are just the
events that knock on their hearts, and their
emotions always tend to answer their hearts'
doors. Nevertheless, if a friend (who doesn't

complain a lot) called you and began complaining, the correct thing to do would be to sharpen them and then the two of you should cast that burden upon the LORD. **Proverbs 27:17:** *Iron sharpens iron; so a man sharpens the countenance of his friend.*

What if they don't want to cast that burden upon the LORD because they feel better now after they've dumped it all on you? It's simple. You educate your friend about the law of transfer, and tell them that you can't carry that load. All you can do is give it to GOD.

But is that all the law of transfer encompasses? No. The law of transfer is the ability (conscious and subconscious) of a human being to transfer their energies, blessings, and pangs to another human being through communication and association. Is this an actual law? Yes, but it's one that has not been studied, nor has it been discovered by mankind. If that's the case, you're probably wondering how I came up with such a law. It's no secret: It's what the LORD has taught and continues to teach us. The scriptures tell us a lot, but most of what we read is hard for us to wrap our minds around because we've been taught to read but not comprehend.

2 Timothy 2:15: *Study to shew thyself approved unto God, a workman that needeth not to be ashamed, rightly dividing the word of truth.*

The Law of Reception

The only way to truly understand the law of
transfer is to understand the law of reception.
Luke 6:38: *Give, and it shall be given unto you;
good measure, pressed down, and shaken
together, and running over, shall men give into
your bosom. For with the same measure that
ye mete withal it shall be measured to you
again.*

When most people read Luke 6:38, they believe
this scripture speaks only of material things,
but we must remember that GOD is SPIRIT.
Much of what HE tells us relates to the realm of
the spirit or is in itself spiritual, but GOD
understands that mankind doesn't always
comprehend the realm of the spirit. Because of
this, many of the scriptures were written in a
way that we could understand. Additionally,

CHRIST oftentimes spoke in parables because of our lack of understanding. But Luke 6:38 goes far beyond our natural comprehension, and so does most of the Bible. That's why we have to seek the Kingdom of GOD by searching the WORD of GOD. When we do, we open ourselves to communicate with GOD, and GOD will give us understanding and increase our knowledge.

Matthew 6:33: *But seek ye first the kingdom of God, and his righteousness; and all these things shall be added unto you.*

1 Corinthians 3:7: *So then neither is he that planteth any thing, neither he that watereth; but God that giveth the increase.*

What Luke 6:38 tells us is that whatever we give to others, we will receive in good measure. Whatever we send out, we will eventually take in, and it will come to us in overflow. In other words, whatever we give, we need to be prepared to receive an abundance of, for every word we speak and everything we do is a seed.

Luke 6:31: *And as ye would that men should do to you, do ye also to them likewise.*

What does all of this mean? It means that, if I want to be blessed, I must first learn to be a blessing. Whatever we are, we attract. Alligators and lions are not attracted to each other because they are not of the same species. Human beings and chimpanzees are not attracted to one another because we are not of the same species. But an alligator will attract another alligator, a lion will attract another lion, a chimpanzee will attract another chimpanzee, and you will attract other human beings. That's how GOD created everything in the earth. Everything in the realm of the earth is attracted to its own kind and can only reproduce after its own kind.

Genesis 1:24: *And God said, Let the earth bring forth the living creature after his kind, cattle, and creeping thing, and beast of the earth after his kind: and it was so.*

If I want to be blessed, I must first learn to be to others what I want to attract to myself. This means I must give up my old way of thinking, come outside of myself and begin to pour out the very thing I've been asking GOD for. Why is that? Why can't I wait until I know it's there before I start pouring out? The answer is obvious. The minute you asked GOD for something, you were supposed to believe HIM for whatever it was you asked HIM for. Once you believe HIM, you have already received your answer from GOD.

2 Corinthians 1:20: *For all the promises of God in him are yea, and in him Amen, unto the glory of God by us.*

Once you understood that GOD'S promises are "yes" and "so be it", you were to do something that the natural mind does not understand in order for you to tap in the realm of the spirit. You were to believe GOD for what you could not see, and if you believe HIM, you will begin to pour out of the abundance of what you've asked HIM for. For example, if you are asking the LORD to increase your finances, you should go out and bless others financially. Even if you can't give a lot, you should give and be sure to give of your lack and not of your abundance. How does one give of their abundance? If you have one hundred dollars that you can sow into someone's life, giving them twenty-five dollars is not giving of your lack; you are giving of your abundance, and because of that, you can't expect much of a harvest. The same measure you give, you will receive. So if you give more, you will receive more, and if you give sparingly, you will receive sparingly. Does this mean the wealthy man who gives a million dollars towards a charity has given more than a poor man who only gave a dollar? Of course not, and CHRIST makes this evident in the story of the widow who gave the two mites.

Mark 12:41-44: *And Jesus sat over against the treasury, and beheld how the people cast money into the treasury: and many that were* *rich cast in much. And there came a certain poor widow, and she threw in two mites, which make a farthing. And he called unto him his disciples, and saith unto them, Verily I say unto you, That this poor widow hath cast more in, than all they which have cast into the treasury: For all they did cast in of their abundance; but she of her want did cast in all that she had, even all her living.*

What did the poor widow give? She gave of her lack. This means that she made a big sacrifice out of faith; whereas, the wealthy people who were giving did not give of their faith; they gave of their substance. Their giving was not a sacrifice; it was a ritualistic act, and with GOD, this makes a huge difference. Consider Abel's offering to GOD. The Bible tells us that Abel gave of his firstlings or first fruit. Cain, on the other hand, just gave. There was no intimacy or love in Cain's offering. It was simply a religious or ritualistic act where he gave because he was supposed to give. Abel gave from his heart, and GOD had respect for Abel's offering, but HE did not have respect for Cain's offering.

The law of reception is that you will receive a sevenfold return on whatever you pour out. If you want to be blessed, then pour out blessings. If you want to see what it's like to have your finances siphoned out of you, then go out and use someone. Additionally, remember that you have to have a heart for giving. If you went out and gave your last with the expectation of receiving a blessing from GOD, then your act was not one of love; it was a ritualistic act, similar to that of Cain's. That's why you'll find many jealous believers running around the church buildings criticizing other believers. They can't understand how one person was blessed suddenly after giving what they perceived to be a little in a short amount of time, when they'd been giving what they believed to be a lot for a long time. After giving of their abundance, they'd waited and waited for whatever it was they'd been praying for, but all they seemed to receive in return was what they put in. What they didn't understand is that they didn't put in a lot. GOD'S not interested in your money. HE can't spend it, nor does HE need it. The earth is HIS and the fullness of it belongs to HIM. GOD is interested in the abundance of your heart, and if you give a lot with little to no faith, it is as if you haven't given a thing. Most people think that money moves GOD when it does not. It's your faith that moves you to give that money, and it is your faith that will place a stamp on that money and cause the news of your giving to reach Heaven. Once GOD sees your faith connected with your seed, HE will then respond with HIS promises: Yea and amen.

Your words can also be used to repel or draw a blessing, just as your words can be used to repel or draw a chastening to you. Words are spirit, and they breathe life into whatever it is you are speaking.

John 6:63: *It is the spirit that quickeneth; the flesh profiteth nothing: the words that I speak unto you, they are spirit, and they are life.*

Have you ever noticed the portion a gossip receives? Most of us have a few relatives who have nothing better to do than sit around and gossip about others. They speak evil, and therefore, they are evil. They speak evil, and therefore, they attract evil and evildoers because we draw after our own kind. That's why gossips are oftentimes surrounded by chaos and troublesome people. Their bellies are never empty of gossip, and they are always the subject of gossip. Their cups run over with what they pour upon others. They keep receiving their portion, and the ones who are religious oftentimes blame the devil for what's been poured upon their lives. That's because they, like most people, don't understand that we are what we put out, and we will continue to grow in that. In everything we do, we start out as a seed, and we continue to grow until we grow up in it and begin to branch out from it. In other words, we get better at being what we are. If you give the ground a seed, it will produce a plant much larger than that seed.

The law of reception is always in motion, and never ceases as long as man continues to give.

Soul Ties & Divorces

Have you ever wondered what a soul tie is, and why so many leaders speak on it? After all, if you search the scriptures, you won't find the actual term "soul ties". That's because the Bible has been translated many times, and even though you may not find the exact word or term you are looking for, you will find words and terms that are synonymous.

So, what exactly is a soul tie and where is the evidence that a soul tie exists? In the Bible, of course. When we join our bodies to other human beings, we become one in the flesh with them, but when we are saved, we become one Spirit in the body of CHRIST. In other words, joining ourselves together in body with another human being is a replica or similar to what we do in the realm of the spirit when we give our lives to the LORD.

Genesis 2:24: *Therefore shall a man leave his father and his mother, and shall cleave unto his wife: and they shall be one flesh.*

1 Corinthians 12:13: *For by one Spirit are we all baptized into one body, whether we be Jews or Gentiles, whether we be bond or free; and have been all made to drink into one Spirit.*

A soul tie is the uniting of two souls, whether that uniting is legal (through GOD-appointed marriage) or illegal (through fornication, adultery, association or unholy matrimony). When we do things GOD'S way, GOD joins our union, and HE is the binding force that keeps it together. When we do things our way, the only thing holding us together is an illegal soul tie. Having an illegal soul tie basically means the enemy has rights to that relationship since it was established on his doctrine: lies.

Ecclesiastes 4:12: *And if one prevail against him, two shall withstand him; and a threefold cord is not quickly broken.*

Mark 10:9: *What therefore God hath joined together, let not man put asunder.*

What exactly happens when a soul tie is established? First off, you must know and understand that a man is an imparter and a woman is a receptor and birther. A man imparts life and whatever is attached to his soul will attach to whatever woman he lies with. That's why men release sperm. They impart their seed into a woman, but a woman does not impart her seed into a man. Once sperm reaches and fertilizes an egg, an embryo begins to form and takes on the form of life. If the egg is not fertilized, it is shed from the woman's womb through a process that we commonly refer to as menstruation. What does this mean? Remember, GOD breathed the breath of life into a man (Adam), but HE created woman (Eve) from the rib of a man; therefore, the ability to impart life is in men, but in order for that life to pass through a woman, it must come from the body of a man.

That's why women are receptors and not imparters. Think of an electrical outlet and a television set. That television set has everything built in it to sustain power and to play whatever man transmits to it, but it won't work without electricity. That's the purpose of the power cord. The power cord allows the power from an electrical outlet to be transmitted into the television set. Once the television is plugged in and turned on, the power from the electrical outlet moves from the cable into the television set, and the set is able to perform as it was designed to perform. This is very similar to how GOD created man and woman. GOD has placed wisdom, love and everything that HE is on the inside of both man and woman, but HE specifically created women to be a help meet to their husbands and to birth life.

Genesis 2:18: *And the LORD God said, It is not good that the man should be alone; I will make him an help meet for him.*

A man is like the extension cord to the television set, but GOD is the power that connects the two. When a man joins himself with a woman, he imparts what GOD has placed in him to that woman, and the two become one. That's why man cannot separate what GOD has brought together. In the realm of the earth, we can divorce one another, but the two shall remain one until GOD says otherwise. The only split between a man and his wife that GOD authorizes is when adultery has been committed, the unbeliever leaves a believer, or through death. Why is this? Adultery is similar to idolatry. Truthfully, idolatry is spiritual adultery against the LORD; whereas, adultery is being unfaithful to the spouse. When a man lies with a woman, he becomes that woman's husband, with or without the vows. If you'll notice, the scriptures speak of the wife committing adultery as being an act that allows a man to divorce her, but when the tables are turned, the Bible does not say that women have the right to divorce their husbands.

Matthew 19:9: *And I say unto you, Whosoever shall put away his wife, except it be for fornication, and shall marry another, committeth adultery: and whoso marrieth her which is put away doth commit adultery.*

Does this mean that a wife cannot divorce her husband? Yes and no.

Why yes? When a man joins himself to a woman, he imparts his soul into that woman, and the two become one flesh. Operating as one flesh is not something we see, of course. They don't become a two-headed couple imprisoned in one physical body. They become one in the eyes of the LORD because the man chose for himself a help meet, whether his choice was legal (through GOD ordained marriage) or illegal (through fornication or adultery). Now, many women get offended when they hear messages like this, but it's actually something that works in the woman's favor. Anytime a man becomes the husband of a woman, he is obligated by GOD to provide for that woman. By abandoning her, he abandons his responsibility, thus putting him in a very bad place with the LORD.

1 Timothy 5:8: *But if any provide not for his own, and especially for those of his own house, he has denied the faith, and is worse than an unbeliever.*

Why no? When an unbelieving husband abandons his wife, if she be a believer, she is free to marry again.

1 Corinthians 7:15: *But if the unbelieving depart, let him depart. A brother or a sister is not under bondage in such cases: but God hath called us to peace.*

Additionally, if the husband is a believing husband, yet he abandons his wife and commits adultery by marrying another woman, either legally or illegally, he becomes worse than an unbeliever with GOD; therefore, the estranged wife can remarry. Of course, this is only allowed if adultery is committed and GOD puts the marriage asunder. This means the wife needs to seek the guidance and approval of GOD before going forward. Irreconcilable differences are not legal defenses with the LORD. Again, this is actually something that works in the woman's favor.

What if the husband hasn't committed adultery, but he's abusive? Can a wife legally divorce him then? No, but she can separate from him. In the scriptures, the Bible tells women not to "depart" or leave their husbands, but it specifically tells husbands not to "put away" or divorce their wives.

1 Corinthians 7:10-11: *And unto the married I command, yet not I, but the Lord, Let not the wife depart from her husband: But and if she depart, let her remain unmarried, or be reconciled to her husband: and let not the husband put away his wife.*

Does this mean that an abused wife must pawn

herself away until her husband turns his life around? After all, that's what it sounds like, and many women who have been abused would growl at such a gesture, but please understand this: A man who is abusive to his wife is more than likely an adulterer. It is very rare, if not impossible, to find a faithful or patient abuser, because abusers love power and are very impatient, since they are driven by dark forces. Abusers are impatient, and that's what drives them to become abusive. In other words, an abuser will eventually abandon his estranged wife, and all too often, it happens relatively quickly. Now, this doesn't mean he will stop harassing his wife. What it does mean is that his desire to have power will eventually drive him into the arms of another woman (or man). One of the things you will see commonly with abusers is that they tend to frequent seedy neighborhoods in search of prostitutes or women they feel they can control, if even for just an hour. Abusers are perverted, meaning, they have turned their hearts away from GOD, and all too often, they are sexually perverted.

Therefore, even though a believing woman can separate from an abuser, she cannot remarry until her husband commits adultery against her. I highly doubt you will ever meet a woman who has been abused by a faithful man. A man must first be faithful to GOD before he can be faithful to his wife, and if he's hitting on or mentally abusing his wife, he's definitely not faithful to GOD.

But what should you do if you've illegally divorced your husband or wife, and married someone else? Is adultery a continuous state? If you have illegally divorced your spouse, you can repent to GOD, and ask HIM to divorce the previous union. Since HE is faithful to forgive us for our sins, adultery is not a continuous state if you've married someone else. The sin remains as long as you don't confess or acknowledge it, therefore, not repenting of it. Please be advised, however, that if you abuse

HIS grace, divorce your spouse (after knowing better), and remarry, your new marriage (in HIS sight) will be considered illegal. As such, the very foundation of that marriage will have to be destroyed if you ever want GOD'S stamp of approval on it. Most marriages do not survive this "tearing down" because the couple then has to find their footing on the WORD of GOD. Most marriages established illegally were entered into by individuals looking to fill their voids and appease their lusts. Once we turn our whole hearts back to GOD, HE fills those voids, and we become stronger against our flesh. This means that the illegal spouse almost becomes useless to us, and that's why it is very important to build your marriage on the unshakable foundation of the WORD.

When a man and a woman become one, the soul of the man joins with the soul of the woman, and the two become one flesh. This is a union that man cannot divide. Man can separate from one another, but when GOD looks at a man who has departed from or put away his legal or illegal wife, GOD sees a married man who is out of order.

The woman is a receptor; therefore, the soul of the man will inhabit her. Every man a woman lies with imparts his soul into her, but it goes much deeper than that. Because she is the wife of multiple men, the Bible refers to her as a harlot. A harlot is a mass burial or pit for souls.

Proverbs 6:26: *For by means of a whorish woman a man is brought to a piece of bread: and the adulteress will hunt for the precious life.*

Proverbs 9:13-18: *A foolish woman is clamorous: she is simple, and knoweth nothing. For she sitteth at the door of her house, on a seat in the high places of the city, To call passengers who go right on their ways: Whoso is simple, let him turn in hither: and as for him that wanteth understanding, she saith to him, Stolen waters are sweet, and bread eaten in secret is pleasant. But he knoweth not that the dead are there; and that her guests are in the* *depths of hell.*

1 Corinthians 6:16: *What? Know ye not that he which is joined to an harlot is one body? For two, saith he, shall be one flesh.*

Because this truth is not well-known, many women go to the LORD asking for HIM to send their GOD-ordained husbands or to just send them a husband. But when the LORD looks upon them, HE sees the impartation of the man or men each particular woman has lain with, because the two are one. Because of this, many women keep having run-ins with their ex-boyfriends, since they are still married to them. To become free from the soul tie, the woman (like the man) must repent to GOD, and allow HIM to put the marriage asunder. This is a process where the woman has to be delivered from the soul tie, and she must start building the foundation for her relationship with the LORD in righteousness. Her marriage will be established on that foundation. Because there isn't a lot of teaching on soul ties and what they really are, many women unknowingly go out and join themselves to other men through dating, kissing and adultery of the heart. Many women fall back into the world's system of dating, but GOD'S way is completely opposite of the world's ... obviously. In dating, a soul tie is oftentimes formed, because dating isn't truly designed to help two people decide if they are right for one another. Dating is designed for two people who are attracted to one another physically to try and see if they have enough in common to give the relationship a try. People can date for years and still divorce because they never consulted the LORD. Courting, on the other hand, is purposeful and designed for believers who want to remain holy. The goal of courting is to commune together in the LORD, while being prayerful about your purpose in one another's life. People can court one week, and if the LORD confirms that the man has found his wife, the two can marry and end up remaining happily married for a lifetime. In dating, there is an automatic assumption that a romantic relationship will be established, and that's why many people kiss on the first or second date. In courting, however, the individuals are seeking GOD before moving forward towards marriage. When a man courts a woman in the LORD, he covers her with prayer, without uncovering her body. If GOD says the two shall not be one in marriage, the couple resumes their lives apart from one another, continually praying for each other as they wait on GOD for their appointed ones. The goal of the man is to not impart himself into a woman whom he cannot provide for, and the goal of the woman is to keep herself from any man who has not first committed himself to an everlasting relationship with GOD through salvation, and a lifetime, earthly relationship with her through marriage.

What is fornication, then? Fornication is not two unmarried people having sex, contrary to popular belief. Fornication is having an illegal marriage through the act of sex. It is to join the flesh before joining together as one in the LORD. It is for a man to uncover a woman in the natural and refuse to cover her in the spirit. In doing so, he causes her to commit adultery.

Consider the rape of Tamar by her brother, Amnon. In those days, it was not a bad thing for a brother to marry a sister if they had different mothers. Amnon was smitten with his sister and decided to rape her. He deceived his father, David, into sending Tamar into his room, and while she was there, he began to force himself on her. Tamar responded by telling Amnon that what he was doing was a shame, and that all he had to do was ask their father for her hand. In doing this, she assures Amnon that David would not keep her from him. In other words, Tamar was telling her brother to honor the marriage laws. In those days, a man (or his family) had to go to the father of the woman he wanted to marry, and he had to ask for her hand in marriage. Amnon did not ask for Tamar's hand. Rape was—and is—a bad thing, of course, but Amnon's act after raping his sister was the real insult to her. He sent her away. In other words, he uncovered her, but refused to cover her. He refused to act as a husband to the woman he'd just joined himself to. In Jewish law, this meant that Tamar could never remarry as long as Amnon lived, and this is why she immediately tore her virgin's garments. To be a married woman and wear the clothes of a virgin was considered an act of deception. When Absalom killed his brother, Amnon, it was because he'd raped Tamar, and he'd dishonored Tamar by not acting as a husband to her. In doing so, Amnon put Tamar to shame, but when Absalom killed Amnon, Tamar was free to remarry and her honor was restored. Tamar and Absalom had the same Mother (Maacah); whereas Absalom was their half brother. His Mother's name was Ahinoam.

Matthew 22:29-30: *Jesus answered and said unto them, Ye do err, not knowing the scriptures, nor the power of God. For in the* resurrection they neither marry, nor are given in marriage, but are as the angels of God in heaven.

1 Corinthians 7:34: *There is difference also between a wife and a virgin. The unmarried woman careth for the things of the Lord, that she may be holy both in body and in spirit: but she that is married careth for the things of the world, how she may please her husband.*

2 Samuel 13:1-20: *And it came to pass after this, that Absalom the son of David had a fair sister, whose name was Tamar; and Amnon the son of David loved her. And Amnon was so vexed, that he fell sick for his sister Tamar; for she was a virgin; and Amnon thought it hard for him to do any thing to her. But Amnon had a friend, whose name was Jonadab, the son of Shimeah David's brother: and Jonadab was a very subtil man. And he said unto him, Why art thou, being the king's son, lean from day to day? wilt thou not tell me? And Amnon said unto him, I love Tamar, my brother Absalom's sister. And Jonadab said unto him, Lay thee* *down on thy bed, and make thyself sick: and when thy father cometh to see thee, say unto him, I pray thee, let my sister Tamar come, and give me meat, and dress the meat in my sight, that I may see it, and eat it at her hand. So Amnon lay down, and made himself sick: and when the king was come to see him, Amnon said unto the king, I pray thee, let Tamar my sister come, and make me a couple of cakes in my sight, that I may eat at her hand.*

Then David sent home to Tamar, saying, Go now to thy brother Amnon's house, and dress him meat. So Tamar went to her brother Amnon's house; and he was laid down. And she took flour, and kneaded it, and made cakes in his sight, and did bake the cakes. And she took a pan, and poured them out before him; but he refused to eat. And Amnon said, Have out all men from me. And they went out every man from him. And Amnon said unto Tamar, Bring the meat into the chamber, that I may eat of thine hand. And Tamar took the cakes which she had made, and brought them into the chamber to Amnon her brother. And when she had brought them unto him to eat, he took hold of her, and said unto her, Come lie with me, my sister. And she answered him, Nay, my brother, do not force me; for no such thing ought to be done in Israel: do not thou this folly. And I, whither shall I cause my shame to go? and as for thee, thou shalt be as one of the fools in Israel. Now therefore, I pray thee, speak unto the king; for he will not withhold me from thee. Howbeit he would not hearken unto her voice: but, being stronger than she, forced her, and lay with her.

Then Amnon hated her exceedingly; so that the hatred wherewith he hated her was greater than the love wherewith he had loved her. And Amnon said unto her, Arise, be gone. And she said unto him, There is no cause: this evil in sending me away is greater than the other that thou didst unto me. But he would not hearken unto her. Then he called his servant that ministered unto him, and said, Put now this woman out from me, and bolt the door after her. And she had a garment of divers colours upon her: for with such robes were the king's daughters that were virgins apparelled. Then his servant brought her out, and bolted the door after her. And Tamar put ashes on her head, and rent her garment of divers colours that was on her, and laid her hand on her head, and went on crying.

And Absalom her brother said unto her, Hath Amnon thy brother been with thee? but hold now thy peace, my sister: he is thy brother; regard not this thing. So Tamar remained desolate in her brother Absalom's house. But when king David heard of all these things, he was very wroth. And Absalom spake unto his brother Amnon neither good nor bad: for Absalom hated Amnon, because he had forced his sister Tamar.

Associations, Communications & Impartations

1 Corinthians 15:33: *Be not deceived: evil communications corrupt good manners.*

You are who you associate with. Whomever you allow into your life, it is that person or those people who will influence your thinking, and our thinking affects our perception and our reception.

Just what did 1 Corinthians 15:33 mean by "evil communications corrupt good manners"? After all, most people claim to be leaders who are not affected by their immoral friends, but in order for that to be true, GOD would have to be doing the impossible: telling a lie. Evil communications is not just having a wicked conversation with someone. To have evil communications is to have an ungodly relationship with that person. Think of the time (if this has ever happened to you) when you had a friend whose season you knew was up in your life. Back in the days, the two of you used to be sin buddies, but now that you are saved and living for the LORD, you find that your friend wants the old you back, but GOD has saved you and renewed your mind. Therefore, the two of you are no longer on the same path. **Amos 3:3:** *Can two walk together, except they are agreed?*

The average person would hold onto that friendship until adversity pulled it apart, because we tend to follow the world's law of loyalty more than we follow the WORD of GOD. Nevertheless, anytime you find yourself around that particular friend, you find yourself doing and saying things you know you should not have done or said. To try and justify the friendship, you throw a few scriptures at your friend and try to coach him or her towards the LORD once again, but they are not going. Do you see what happened? Instead of you bringing your friend towards the LORD, your friend is leading you towards his or her lord; the force in which he or she serves. Because of this, you become double-minded. You are now going between two paths trying to maintain the most important relationships in your lives: the relationship with who you can see (the friend) and the relationship with who you can't see (the LORD).

James 1:8: *A double minded man is unstable in all his ways.*

Every relationship you have with another human being is either evil communication or righteous communication. Your relationships are either leading you towards the LORD or leading you away from HIM.

Most people who get saved come into

salvation with those old friends and old mindsets, because our minds don't change once we get saved. We still have to be transformed by the renewing of our minds, and until this happens, we will still find ourselves attracted to and attracting people who are headed in the opposite direction. As our love for the LORD grows, we will stop trying to divide our loyalties between our old relationships and our new relationship with the FATHER. Our minds will change, thus causing us to no longer agree with our friends, and this is where our paths often fork off.

But there are some people who are so loyal to the people in their lives that they refuse to allow their minds to change. They simply embrace salvation, but they refuse to embrace GOD. They stand on the side of this war with the world, and against the church. They hate holiness and they believe anyone who radiates holiness has a "holier than thou" complex. Their favorite quotes are:

Judge yet not!
Only GOD can judge me!
I remember when you used to...
GOD knows my heart!

Because of their double-mindedness, they have not truly embraced salvation, because they aren't serving the living GOD. Instead, they have embraced an image of what and who they think GOD is, and the image is not HIM. It is an idol that they've erected in their hearts. They have rejected the living GOD to pursue an imagined god; one who allows them to bask in their sins and disregard HIS Holy WORD. In trying to maintain a friendship with someone who does not love or fear the LORD, they have chosen to continue on the path that once led them towards destruction, but the only difference is that they oftentimes veer off that path to go to the church building.

So what is one to do with those old friends who want no part of GOD or who are grafted into religion but not holiness? What if that person is you? Should you call those friends and tell them that you can no longer be their friend because of their lifestyles and mindsets? That's not necessary if you live the way GOD told you to live. If you refuse to sin with them or allow them to sin around you, they will disassociate from you because the two of you no longer agree. You will find that the phone calls and visits will become less and less. You are now different creatures, and as such, the only thing you have in common is that you possess a mortal body.

Whatever you allow into your ears, it is that thing that will eventually get into your heart. Even if you do not agree with something someone said, eventually their words will become familiar to you and slither into your heart. This means that we become one in our thinking and journeys with the people we associate with. Anytime we invite or allow someone into our lives, we become members of one body with them. That body isn't a physical body that one can see; that body is called purpose, and if we do not disconnect ourselves from that body, we will enter into the everlasting joy or torments reserved for that body. After all, we can't serve two gods.

1 Samuel 18:1: *And it came to pass, when he had made an end of speaking unto Saul, that the soul of Jonathan was knit with the soul of David, and Jonathan loved him as his own soul.*

Mark 9:43-48: *And if thy hand offend thee, cut it off: it is better for thee to enter into life maimed, than having two hands to go into hell, into the fire that never shall be quenched: Where their worm dieth not, and the fire is not quenched. And if thy foot offend thee, cut it off: it is better for thee to enter halt into life, than having two feet to be cast into hell, into the fire that never shall be quenched: Where their worm dieth not, and the fire is not quenched. And if thine eye offend thee, pluck it out: it is better for thee to enter into the kingdom of God with one eye, than having two eyes to be cast into hell fire: Where their worm*

dieth not, and the fire is not quenched.
Luke 16:13: *No servant can serve two masters: for either he will hate the one, and love the other; or else he will hold to the one, and despise the other. Ye cannot serve God and mammon.*

Prayers & Impartations

Have you ever had someone who offered (or threatened) to pray for you? When someone offers to pray for us, we oftentimes feel appreciative because we believe their gesture to mean that they want the best for us. Howbeit, many people who offer to pray for us don't have our best interest in mind. Sometimes, they simply do not agree with you in relation to what you are praying for, or they don't think you deserve what you've been praying for. Because of this, many people pray against what you've asked GOD for. Should we be concerned? Of course not. A prayer from a dark and misguided heart is a prayer that GOD won't hear or answer. Nevertheless, what should concern us is who and what they are praying to.

In the United States of America, Christianity is one of the largest lifestyles, oftentimes, referred to as a "religion." Of course, Christianity isn't a religion; it is a way of life. Nevertheless, with the large number of people who claim to be Christian in this country, there are countless churches erected each year to house the growing congregations. But we'd be in the dark if we allowed ourselves to believe that every one of those churches is GOD-filled. Instead, many of those churches are pagan-fronts erected by the enemy to draw in unsuspecting believers. These churches are run by wolves who have learned the art of mimicking real men and women of GOD. These dark souls are devil-filled and hell-bent on getting what they want. They see having and running a church as a platform to help them feel empowered and to rob a lost people of their wages. They pervert the people by feeding them perverted doctrine (lies). They lay hands on their members and make demonic impartations into each person who dares to allow them to lay hands on them. How is this done? It's simple. Every church you enter has a head, and each member is a part of the body of that church. Anything that's wrong with the head will be what's wrong with the body.

2 Corinthians 11:12-15: *But what I do, that I will do, that I may cut off occasion from them which desire occasion; that wherein they glory, they may be found even as we. For such are false apostles, deceitful workers, transforming themselves into the apostles of Christ. And no marvel; for Satan himself is transformed into an angel of light. Therefore it is no great thing if his ministers also be transformed as the ministers of righteousness; whose end shall be according to their works.*

Matthew 7:15: *Beware of false prophets, which come to you in sheep's clothing, but inwardly they are ravening wolves.*

But what if the members truly love and fear the LORD? Are they influenced and led astray by wolves, or will GOD intervene and bring them in the way of righteousness? The answers are in the scriptures.

Isaiah 9:16: *For the leaders of this people cause them to err; and they that are led of them are destroyed.*

1 Corinthians 10:13: *There hath no temptation taken you but such as is common to man: but God is faithful, who will not suffer you to be tempted above that ye are able; but will with the temptation also make a way to escape, that ye may be able to bear it.*

Revelations 2:20: *Notwithstanding I have a few things against thee, because thou sufferest that woman Jezebel, which calleth herself a prophetess, to teach and to seduce my servants to commit fornication, and to eat things sacrificed unto idols.*

First, to love the LORD, we have to know the LORD. Howbeit, many people who claim to be Christian don't really know CHRIST. They know the pagan image that they've been introduced to, but they don't know the true and living

GOD. Because of this, many people who think they are believers are actually unbelievers. How so? They serve the image that's been introduced to them, but they have not truly been introduced to the LORD. This is evident in the celebration of many pagan rituals such as Easter (instead of CHRIST'S resurrection), the traditional celebration of Christmas, and the celebration of Halloween. Therefore, we hear and know that a Christian cannot be inhabited or possessed by a devil, but many people end up becoming the houses of demons because they are not truly saved.

Luke 13:26-27: *Then shall you begin to say, We have eaten and drunk in your presence, and you have taught in our streets. But he shall say, I tell you, I know not where you come from; depart from me, all you workers of iniquity.*

Then again, there are many people who are saved, but they are being misled by entering into buildings not designed for GOD. Are they unsaved? No. Many know the LORD, but have not learned enough about HIM to discern who is for HIM and who is against HIM. As each child of GOD matures in HIM, they begin to recognize HIS voice, and that's why many people end up suffering from what is commonly referred to as "church hurt." Church hurt is oftentimes a term used to describe a person being betrayed by the members, and, more often than not, the leaders of the churches they were once members of. Because these children are seeking GOD with their hearts, they are protected by GOD since they are inhabited by the HOLY SPIRIT. Therefore, they are not demonically possessed, but they can be demonically influenced until they learn better. When one is a babe in CHRIST, he or she oftentimes does not trust or recognize the voice of the HOLY SPIRIT, but as each man or woman grows up in the LORD, they began to recognize HIS voice. As they begin to know HIM, they begin to recognize when they are being led in a way that's opposite of HIM.

When they attempt to question the ministry or back away from it, they are often accused of being demon-possessed, talked about or ex-communicated from the very ministry they once loved and trusted with their souls. Therefore, oftentimes, church hurt equates to a believer who's just awakened to the truth while seated in the midst of liars.

What is to be said of this? It's simple. Devils do transfer into unbelievers, but they can only attach to, follow and influence believers. That is, until those believers finally start recognizing and listening to the voice of GOD.

So what exactly happens when a false teacher lays hands on a person and makes an impartation into that person? If the person is truly a believer, the impartation is done in the soulish realm, similar to what happens when a man imparts himself into a woman. A soul tie is established between the imparter and the person receiving the impartation. This means that whatever is attached to the person making the impartation attaches itself to the person receiving the impartation, but only in the soulish realm. If the person believes more in the leader than they do in the LORD, they are unbelievers, since we can't serve two masters. They have not yet met the LORD; instead, they've heard about HIM and HIS marvelous works. Of course, if the person receiving the impartation is an unbeliever, then the impartation can result in demonic possession. The difference is:

- Only unbelievers can fall victim to demonic possession.

- Believers can fall victim to demonic oppression and depression, but not possession.

Possession takes place on the inside; whereas, oppression takes place on the outside. Depression is bringing in what's on the outside into the inside of one's heart. Depression happens when we receive the lies as truth, and our soul begins to lament and hunger after the truth.

What about prayers? What happens when we ask someone to pray for us? When we ask someone to pray for us, we simply give them permission to pray to their god for us. If they happen to be unbelievers, there is no telling where their prayers are going, but they are definitely not reaching Heaven. Anytime you ask someone to pray for you, you will open yourself up to receive the answer of that prayer. This means that if the person who is praying for you is praying to the image of a false god, whether they know it or not, they are praying to devils. When you receive those prayers, you open your home up to whatever and whomever they've reached out to. Please remember that devils do attach themselves to the minds of believers, but they cannot possess them.

Finally, always look at the fruit (or works) of a person. A man's mouth can lie, but whatever he is will always be revealed through his actions. If his love for his brothers and sisters in the LORD is not evident, you're likely dealing with a wolf. Always look for the love of GOD in a person, and don't hang on to their every word.

1 John 4:20: *If a man say, I love God, and hateth his brother, he is a liar: for he that loveth not his brother whom he hath seen, how can he love God whom he hath not seen?*
1 Corinthians 6:19-20: *What? Know ye not that your body is the temple of the Holy Ghost which is in you, which ye have of God, and ye are not your own? For ye are bought with a price: therefore glorify God in your body, and in your spirit, which are God's.*

1 John 4:4: *Ye are of God, little children, and have overcome them: because greater is he that is in you, than he that is in the world.*

How do we overcome the enemy? How do we learn to discern GOD'S voice from the voice of the enemy? We do this through having an actual relationship with GOD. We initiate a relationship with HIM by seeking the Kingdom of GOD and all its righteousness; meaning, we seek to know HIM intimately. We search the WORD, and we adjust our lives accordingly. As we seek to know GOD more, we stop searching for the pleasures of life, and we seek to please GOD more. Our relationship with the FATHER becomes one that is real, and not religious. We stop worshipping Sunday and we start worshipping the LORD. We stop reverencing the church building, and we come to understand that we are the temples of the HOLY SPIRIT. The issue with many people is that they go to church and seek the approval of their leaders and the church's members. Many people do not stray outside of what they were taught, even when what they were taught is false. Many people are invited to seek the truth by GOD, but refuse to go outside of what they know. That's because new information challenges old information, and most people fear being forced to choose between two doctrines. No one wants to believe that they've had it all wrong. Everyone wants to believe that they are serving the LORD, and it's easier to get a man to question the truth than it is to get him to question what he's been taught. Additionally, it's easier to get a man to rebuke a person who brings the truth than it is to get that same man to rebuke the leader or the religion he's learned to idolize.

1 John 4:1: *Beloved, believe not every spirit, but try the spirits whether they are of God: because many false prophets are gone out into the world.*

Jeremiah 29:13: *And ye shall seek me, and find me, when ye shall search for me with all your heart.*

Matthew 6:33: *But seek ye first the kingdom of God, and his righteousness; and all these things shall be added unto you.*

Proverbs 16:25: *There is a way that seemeth*

right unto a man, but the end thereof are the ways of death.

John 10:27-30: *My sheep hear my voice, and I know them, and they follow me: And I give unto them eternal life; and they shall never perish, neither shall any man pluck them out of my hand. My Father, which gave them me, is greater than all; and no man is able to pluck them out of my Father's hand. I and my Father are one.*

Matthew 7:16-20: *Ye shall know them by their fruits. Do men gather grapes of thorns, or figs of thistles? Even so every good tree bringeth forth good fruit; but a corrupt tree bringeth forth evil fruit. A good tree cannot bring forth evil fruit, neither can a corrupt tree bring forth good fruit. Every tree that bringeth not forth good fruit is hewn down, and cast into the fire. Wherefore by their fruits ye shall know them.*

Romans 1:25: *Who changed the truth of God into a lie, and worshipped and served the creature more than the Creator, who is blessed for ever. Amen.*

Familiar Spirits & Relationships

We've all heard the term "familiar" spirit, but most people don't exactly know what a familiar spirit is. The term "familiar" gives us a little insight, but not enough information. A familiar spirit is a spirit that has traveled through a family generation to generation. For example, most soothsayers or witches have familiar spirits. You will find that many people who are into witchcraft picked up their "gifts" from one or both of their parents. Additionally, familiar spirits do lie dormant in some people, but may show up strongly in their children.

The word "familiar" is derived from the word "family". Google defines "familiar" as:
1. commonly or generally known or seen.
2. well-acquainted; thoroughly conversant.

3. informal; easygoing; unceremonious; unconstrained.

4. closely intimate or personal: a familiar friend; to be on familiar terms.

5. unduly intimate; too personal; taking liberties; presuming.

What do all of these definitions of "familiar" tell us? They tell us that to be familiar with something or someone is to be personally acquainted with that thing or person. It means to have a relationship with that thing or person. Therefore, a familiar spirit is a spirit that has a relationship with a person, whether that relationship was initiated by the person in question, or if it came through family lineage. Either way, a familiar spirit is a spirit that is very common.

Familiar spirits are like diseases. They are contagious and often spread through associations, sex, religious impartations, sorcery and families. What makes a familiar spirit a common spirit is the fact that it often goes by undetected. Familiar spirits oftentimes don't control people; instead, they influence them. Familiar spirits attach themselves to the minds of their hosts. They understand that if a man believes their report, as opposed to the WORD of GOD, that man will forfeit his blessings. Familiar spirits were once angels in Heaven, but now are fallen angels. They are a part of the third of angels who rebelled against GOD. Because of this, they understand the makeup of mankind, and what we need to get us through each day. A familiar spirit's goal is to get its hosts to eject GOD from certain areas of their lives and hearts by rejecting the truth. In doing so, each host creates a void within themselves; a void that has to be filled. When a void is created, a lying spirit (which is oftentimes a part of the familiar legion) will offer the person it's trying to attach to solutions and void-fillers. Once that person bites the bait, they create a relationship with the familiar spirits.

Additionally, when a man picks up a thinking pattern, he can no longer associate himself with others who do not think like him. Because of this, he will seek and be drawn to individuals who are like him, or individuals who have voids that he's interested in filling. That's why an abusive and power-starved man can easily identify a woman who has low self-esteem. Having low self-esteem means she's been lied to and she's accepted the lies she was told. Nevertheless, she still desires to be married and loved; therefore, she lowers her standards and accepts any man Satan sends her way. During her courtship with the man who has familiar spirits, she too picks up those spirits through a soul tie. Because the man comes in and operates as her head, she knowingly or unknowingly submits herself to whatever he is in submission to. When and if that man abandons her, a new void is created; one that was greater than the last void. Because she's now had a relationship with the spirits that came to her through the man she was dating, she will begin to seek familiar spirits, oftentimes unknowingly. That's why you'll find women who tend to be attracted to a certain type of man. The issue isn't that she's truly attracted to the man; she's attracted to the spirits within that man.

After a woman has been abandoned several times, she may become desperate to get the void-fillers she feels she was getting in those relationships. In other words, it is possible (and very common) for someone to become addicted to having spirits in or attached to them. Afraid of losing touch with their void-fillers again, many women turn to witchcraft. In her search, her head (soul) has been uncovered many times, but no man covered or protected her from the spirits that are now calling her soul their home. Every man she has slept with has uncovered her body, just as they've uncovered her soul. When a man undresses a woman, it represents "exposure." But when a husband undresses his wife, he covers her with his love and prayers; therefore, he doesn't expose her; he protects her. When an illegal husband undresses a woman, he exposes her, and this represents the exposing of her head (soul). When a woman's head is uncovered, she becomes a public breeding ground for devils and powers. That's why it is VERY important to be careful who you allow to pray for or lay hands on you. Many women who refer to themselves as prophetesses are actually exposed souls who are tapped into familiar spirits. Of course, the same goes for men.

1 Corinthians 11:5-10: *But every woman that prayeth or prophesieth with her head uncovered dishonoureth her head: for that is even all one as if she were shaven. For if the woman be not covered, let her also be shorn: but if it be a shame for a woman to be shorn or shaven, let her be covered. For a man indeed ought not to cover his head, forasmuch as he is the image and glory of God: but the woman is the glory of the man. For the man is not of the*

woman; but the woman of the man. Neither
was the man created for the woman; but the
woman for the man. For this cause ought the
woman to have power on her head because of
the angels.

1 Corinthians 11:3: But I would have you
know, that the head of every man is Christ; and
the head of the woman is the man; and the
head of Christ is God.

What does these scripture tell us? Let's first
talk about men, since a man is the head of a
woman. A man who is not saved is a man with
an uncovered head (spirit).

Proverbs 25:28: He that hath no rule over his
own spirit is like a city that is broken down, and
without walls.

When a man is unsaved, he is under the Old
Testament law; therefore, he is accursed. When
an unsaved man lies with a woman, he
becomes the head of that woman, and she
begins to walk under his covering. In this case,

he is not covered, but exposed to the law and everything that came with it. Anytime a man uncovers a woman, he exposes her to whatever or whomever he serves. Even if a man is saved, yet he fornicates with a woman, he exposes that woman to the law. How so? Because in fornicating with her, he gave in to the law of his flesh. He did not honor GOD; therefore, he has rejected his covering to submit to the law of his flesh. That's why it is very important for him to repent and turn his heart back to GOD. Fornication is an act of perversion, and perversion is not always sexual. To be perverted means to be contaminated or turned away from GOD. It means the original intent or makeup of a thing has been altered so that it no longer works the way the CREATOR created it to work. Therefore, when a man is perverted, his thinking has been altered, and he no longer works the way the CREATOR created HIM to work. To repent is not to apologize, but it is to truly be sorry and turn one's heart back to GOD. To repent means to recover one's head.

The act of bowing down in prayer and worship represents submission.

Next, what we learn from 1 Corinthians 11:5-10 is that a woman who prays or prophesies with her head uncovered is out of order. In the Old Testament, we had to perform certain works to redeem or justify ourselves, but now that we are under the New Covenant, CHRIST is our covering. A woman covering her head with a cloth (as done in the Old Testament) represented her soul being covered. Nowadays, women don't have to wear material coverings on their heads. Instead, a wife must be covered by her husband after he has made a vow with GOD to cover her. In order to walk under the covering of CHRIST, we must follow the new law. That is to love GOD with all of our hearts, soul and strength, and to love our brethren as we love ourselves. GOD said that if we love HIM, we are to keep HIS commandments. We know that we were redeemed from the curse of the law, but does this mean that the old law has been removed? No. It means that the law has been established. In other words, you wouldn't kill a man if you loved him as you love yourself. You wouldn't lie to someone if you loved them as you love yourself. You would not commit adultery against someone you truly love as you love yourself. Now, if you love yourself more than you love your spouse, you will commit adultery against them. That's why CHRIST said that we are to love one another as we love ourselves. In doing this, we refrain from doing or saying things to others that we don't want done or said to us. In other words, love will make a man cover his wife instead of uncovering his girlfriend. Love will make a woman retain the power over her head until a man promises to GOD (through marriage vows) to cover her after he uncovers her. As a matter of fact, before a man lies with his wife, he should cover her, and before he covers her, he must be covered by CHRIST through salvation.

Familiar spirits transfer through many avenues, but, of course, illegal sex is their favorite highway. Many familiar spirits appear to people in their dreams in the form of a person they are familiar with. For example, if you are a man and you dream that you've had intercourse with your ex-girlfriend, the dream is not a revelatory dream about your ex-girlfriend; it is a familiar spirit attempting to open up your mind. Many people think spirits can attach themselves to people through their dreams, but this isn't true. A man's will and emotions are directly attached to his heart. His will is the highway that leads to his heart; therefore, a devil cannot access his heart or soul unless he wills it in one way or another. One way for him to will it in is to fantasize about having sex with his ex-girlfriend or another woman, because even thinking about sex with someone you are not legally married to is a sin before GOD. It is considered adultery, even if you aren't a married man because you've strayed away from GOD in your mind; therefore, you are committing adultery with the woman you're fantasizing about in your heart. Of course, the sin is not imputed to her if she does not fantasize about you. If she has covered herself in seductive garments, her sin is that she allowed herself to be a tool to lead men away from GOD in the direction of Satan. In this, she is referred to as a seductress. To seduce means "to lead astray." Of course, the word "stray" is derived from the word "astray." For example, when we speak of a stray dog, what we are saying is that the dog is homeless. He is a creature without a master or a creature who has abandoned his master. When a woman seduces a man, she is attempting to lead him away from his Master (GOD). A man without a Master will always make sin his master.

Matthew 5:28: *But I say unto you, That whosoever looketh on a woman to lust after her hath committed adultery with her already in his heart.*

Romans 6:13: *Neither yield ye your members*

as instruments of unrighteousness unto sin: but yield yourselves unto God, as those that are alive from the dead, and your members as instruments of righteousness unto God.
Romans 6:16: *Know ye not, that to whom ye yield yourselves servants to obey, his servants ye are to whom ye obey; whether of sin unto death, or of obedience unto righteousness?*

Familiar spirits like to hide in plain sight, because man is oftentimes blinded by his own lusts, and we live in a time where people shun holiness. For example, horoscopes are tales told by familiar spirits through the souls who host them. Anytime a person reads a horoscope, they open themselves up to familiar spirits. That's why soothsayers and witches are oftentimes referred to as channelers. They are like cable cords plugged into the power of darkness, and anytime a person comes to them for a reading, the soothsayer or witch channels the spirits attached to the person looking for the reading. Those spirits then relay to the channeler what they've witnessed or what they plan to bring to pass in that person's life. Many people go to sorcerers looking for information about their dead relatives; howbeit, as Christians we all should know that the dead no longer walk the earth. Once their spirit leaves their body, they no longer have permission to walk about the earth realm. So how is a person who has never met another human being or their family members able to tell that person about their lives and the lives of their dead relatives? The answer is obvious. They are surrounded by or filled with familiar spirits, and again, those spirits have oftentimes traveled generation to generation for thousands of years. Therefore, they met, inhabited, seduced, attached themselves to and led astray many of our dead relatives when they were alive. The dead do not walk the earth. Instead, familiar spirits disguise themselves as loved ones who have passed on because it keeps the people who love them from seeking deliverance from them.

Additionally, many people in grieving open themselves up to familiar spirits in an attempt to seek closure when someone they love passes away.

Lastly, familiar spirits anticipate many of the holidays we've come to love. That's because the traditional celebration of many major holidays is rooted in paganism. For example, the traditional celebration of Easter is pagan, and started as the worship of the pagan goddess Ishtar. As believers, we shouldn't celebrate Easter (Ishtar translated); we should celebrate the Resurrection of JESUS CHRIST. The traditional celebration of Christmas is pagan. Many of the things incorporated in these holidays are rooted in the celebration of devils, and anytime a person celebrates a holiday using pagan practices, they conjure up familiar spirits (the devils associated with those practices). Because many have come to love the traditional celebration of popular holidays such as Christmas, Easter and Halloween, they refuse to give them up, even once they realize they are pagan. Many claim that "GOD knows their hearts" and that they aren't celebrating as the pagans once celebrated. Many blind souls call on the name of the LORD while practicing pagan rituals. Because of this, many believers do not know GOD. Instead, they worship the image of who they were told HE was, but they have no actual relationship with HIM, for HE said that those who worship HIM must worship HIM in Spirit and in Truth. In other words, we can't go under the covering of lies and pagan practices and attempt to serve or worship HIM.

One reason familiar spirits often go by undetected is they influence a person to create strongholds or habits in their lives. Bad habits are oftentimes familiar strongholds that we've become comfortable with. For example, an obese man who habitually eats the wrong foods as a way of comforting himself has a familiar spirit. What that spirit is doing is helping the man to self destruct by feeding his flesh and starving his spirit. He strengthens his flesh against himself, and as his flesh becomes stronger, the man becomes weaker. After a while, he begins to yield himself to slothfulness and depression. The only comfort he seems to find is in the foods that are slowly killing him, but because he doesn't know any other way to go, he continues down the destructive, but familiar, path that Satan has introduced him to. When a way of escape is presented to him, he will likely ignore it because his flesh is strong against him. Diet, exercise and deliverance begin to look like villains to him. He is unaware that his flesh is attracted to death.

How do you overcome familiar spirits? It's simple. If you are saved, take authority over your mind and life. Repent to GOD for going astray and get back on the path that GOD has created for you through JESUS CHRIST. Below are ten tips to help you break the strongholds associated with familiar spirits.

　　1. Repent to GOD. Repentance is the first

step to deliverance. Of course, if you are unsaved, you need to get to know GOD and get saved.

2. Confess your sins to GOD, and if HE gives you a friend you can speak with, tell him or her about it as well so he or she can act as your accountability partner.

3. Create a log for yourself, and log every time you are tempted to go back into your old ways.

4. If you give in and sin against the LORD, repent again and again until living a righteous lifestyle becomes a habit.

5. Make righteous living a priority, but pay for your sins. Find a charity and give them a certain amount of money every time you fall into your old habits. For example, let's say you are trying to break the stronghold of procrastination, so you've decided to start that business GOD told you to start. You create a five day schedule for yourself, and each day,

you are committing two hours towards developing and maintaining your business. One day, you wake up and realize your old mindset is paying you a visit. It wants to come back home. On this particular day, you find yourself feeling slothful, and you decide not to do any work that day. Penalize yourself, and make it hurt. It is better to already have a pre-determined penalization fee, one that gets your attention and serves as a blessing to others. If you give a little, it won't sting enough to get your attention. Give to the point where you feel you won't have any extra money to have fun with. Anytime you learn to discipline yourself, you save GOD the task of having to discipline or chasten you.

6. Find several people who are willing to walk that journey with you and act as accountability partners. Oftentimes, when we have help or partners,

whatever challenge we're facing doesn't seem so intimidating.

7. Every time a thought comes in that goes against GOD, rebuke it. Don't submit to it, and definitely don't consider it.

8. Speak to whatever is attacking, attaching to or attempting to attach itself to your mind. Take authority over it by binding it and casting it into the pit (spirit prison) until the Day of Judgment.

9. Praise God when you are tempted. The enemy hates the sound of true praise, and will often flee when he sees you going into the presence of GOD.

10. Pray in the Spirit anytime you find yourself being tempted. Please know that praying in the Spirit scares the enemy as he does not understand what you are praying. Additionally, praying in the Spirit builds you up, and tears down your flesh.

To break away from a familiar spirit, you must

break your relationship with it. When we become saved, we become new creatures in CHRIST. We can't go back to our old ways, because, in doing so, it's like reconciling with the enemy. It's like divorcing Satan, but still visiting him from time-to-time for a rendezvous in the dark while you are married to GOD. You can't serve two masters. Whatever you submit your members (body) to, it is that very thing which you serve.

Romans 12:1: *I beseech you therefore, brethren, by the mercies of God, that ye present your bodies a living sacrifice, holy, acceptable unto God, which is your reasonable service.*

2 Corinthians 5:17: *Therefore if any man be in Christ, he is a new creature: old things are passed away; behold, all things are become new.*

Matthew 9:16-17: *No man putteth a piece of new cloth unto an old garment, for that which is put in to fill it up taketh from the garment, and the rent is made worse. Neither do men* *put new wine into old bottles: else the bottles break, and the wine runneth out, and the bottles perish: but they put new wine into new bottles, and both are preserved.*

Negativity & Unforgiveness

Have you ever wondered why negative people tend to spread their negativity like an infectious disease? Imagine a party of five individuals laughing and talking about the joys of life. Suddenly, one of their negative friends walks up and isn't exactly in the joyful mood. Instead, that friend stands by with a smug look as the rest of the individuals laugh and try to hold on to the joy they feel they are about to be robbed of. Even though everyone tried to maintain their smiles, they couldn't help but feel uneasy. Suddenly, Mr. Negativity decides to speak, and he's complaining about some crazed driver who almost ran him off the road. Just as it seems he's about to end his story, he suddenly starts another story that involves him being in the checkout line at a local supermarket. In this particular story, he is yet again the victim of another rude human being. As it turns out, the person who was in line in front of him had several transactions to make, and ended up writing a check for each transaction. Everyone tries to brush off the negative energy, but Mr. Negativity stands by and is determined to shift everyone's mood because he's not in a happy place. He doesn't like the fact that everyone is laughing, so he interrupts every person's story to tell another negative story. We've all had or have that negative friend who seems to be a magnet for evil, and when we see them coming our way, we oftentimes try to avoid them if we want to keep our joy. After all, every time you talk with this person, you have to tell a story of when you were victimized by something or someone because they are never in the mood for happy stories. They want to complain, and they want someone else to complain to, just as they always have something or someone to complain about.

Just what is the deal with negative people?
Why can't they see the joys of life? Why is it
that they seem to speak one language, and
that language is called complaining? As a man
thinks, so is he (*See Proverbs 23:7*). A man who
is full of darkness can't see the joys of life.
Because he is blind, he is only stimulated by
what he feels or hears. Of course, it goes much
deeper than that.

GOD told us not to let the sun set on our
anger. The reason HE said this is because
anger is not something we are supposed to
carry in our hearts. Anger should be a reaction
and not a lifestyle. It's okay to be angry, but
the Bible tells us not to sin when we are angry.
When we don't forgive one another for our
trespasses, anger and wrath begin to seep into
our hearts, and whatever finds its way into our
hearts will shape our minds and lifestyles.
When we are angered or hurt by someone,
temptation always stands by to offer us a way
to pacify our anger and punish the person

who's made us angry. In other words, anger begins to turn into wrath.

GOD has given us ways to get past anger, but we often find ourselves wanting to punish the people who've hurt us. Because of this, many people bypass GOD'S instructions to exact revenge against others. This is done especially with those closest to us because they are close enough to us to repeatedly step on our toes. For example, let's say that your brother borrowed money from you, and now, he's refusing to pay you back. GOD instructed us to forgive our brethren, but the enemy tells us that, if we let it go, our brother will continue to take advantage of us; therefore, we need to teach him a lesson. Because of this, many people begin to speak with other family members about what their dishonest brother has done, and if they can find a way to get their money back—whether it's by honest or dishonest means—many will take that opportunity. That's because we like to play

GOD, but wrath is something man cannot hold or bear.

Because your brother took the money from you, you decide that you are angry with him and the two of you will no longer speak with one another. For years, you carry that anger in your heart, but you don't realize that you're operating in unforgiveness because you've learned to function with that anger. Until you deal with that hurt and forgive your brother for his debt, you will be a magnet that attracts evil. Why is that? Because we attract what we are. If you are a man walking in unforgiveness, you are an unforgiven man. It doesn't matter how nice you are, how many people you help or how many times you go to church, if you have not submitted your whole heart to GOD, you are not a servant of HIS. Of course, many people would shun such teaching. That is, until they read the entire Bible and understand that anytime we don't forgive one another for our trespasses, GOD cannot forgive us. If GOD does not forgive us, that means we are guilty, damned, dark, lost, unsaved, hell-bound ... and, of course, the list goes on and on. In order to serve GOD and walk in the grace of GOD, we must extend grace to one another. Anytime someone wrongs us, we shouldn't become wrathful and angry. Instead, we are to see those moments as teaching moments. Each lesson comes to tell us how close or how far someone should be from our hearts. For example, if you have a dishonest brother, chances are you need to distance yourself from him in love, but not through unforgiveness. This means that your separation from him is not done out of anger or an attempt to hurt him; it's done because you are protecting yourself from the darkness that lives in him. Nevertheless, many people are still carrying around those burdens that were cast upon them by other humans.

Anytime a person hurts you, the correct way to manage your heart is to prohibit the issue from entering your heart. Instead, the LORD told us to cast our burdens upon HIM. If you meditate on what was done to you, it will get into your heart and become your heart's condition. That's when you'll walk about the earth as a negative force, sucking the joy out of everyone who dares to allow you near their hearts. If you allow gossips to come around and constantly resurrect that situation for the sake of having a conversation, that situation will become your new home. That's how people end up becoming obsessed with situations and come to the point where they can't seem to talk about anything else but the latest news in those situations or in those people's lives.

People are often locked into unforgiveness by wrath, and wrath always provokes vengeance. Anytime you come in contact with a negative person, you have come in contact with a person who has a lot of burdens they have yet to cast upon the LORD. In other words, they are walking in unforgiveness. Anytime you associate yourself with an individual who is burdened by unforgiveness, that person will cast some of that burden upon you day after day. Everywhere they go, they won't be the life of the party; instead, they will be the vampire who sucks the life out of the party. And because they've learned to function in unforgiveness, they oftentimes don't see the need for deliverance.

Negative energy is the result of letting the sun set on one's anger. Anytime wrath is allowed to stay with us overnight, it moves in and decides to make our hearts its permanent home. Unforgiveness creates an environment of strife, and strife opens the door for the enemy.

James 3:16: *For where envying and strife is, there is confusion and every evil work.*

Additionally, unforgiveness is directly linked to a haughty spirit (the spirit behind pride). Anger is a haughty spirit's favorite tool designed to lure us away from GOD and bring us back into our flesh. This is when we step into ourselves in an attempt to confront and correct whomever we feel has provoked us. Once we are back in our flesh, we find the old comforts of the flesh awaiting us. Suddenly, we realize that we can handle many of the situations we've handed to GOD much faster. All we need is will and know-how, and we believe we can fix our lives. Of course, this is a haughty spirit (pride) seducing us with its lies. This is why we cannot allow wrath to camp out overnight at our homes or in our hearts.

Everything in the realm of the earth and the realm of the spirit only draws whatever it relates to. Darkness can never have a relationship with the light, just as unforgiveness can never have a relationship with our hearts. Unforgiveness is like an abusive lover; one who is wrathful, vengeful, blood-thirsty and drunk with power. Unforgiveness will always beat the heart of whosoever lets it in until that person is delivered or until their hearts give way from its injuries. Negativity is simply the evidence of unforgiveness; it's when unforgiveness is comfortable enough to show itself in the form of negative energy.

How can one be delivered from unforgiveness? The answer is obvious: forgive. The way we forgive others is by looking past their sins to see their good. Also, it's easier to forgive someone for their trespasses against us when we consider our trespasses against GOD and how HE has forgiven us time and time again. But if you have trouble forgiving someone, give your heart to GOD and ask HIM for a new one. Ask HIM to put forgiveness in your heart and to cause you to walk in that forgiveness. Also, incorporate the person who's hurt you into your prayers as often as you can. Pray for them and not against them. As you extend love to them, GOD will extend HIS love into your heart. Again, you attract what you are, and when you display love, you attract GOD, for GOD is love.

Imaginations & Realities

We all have imaginations, but there are two types of imaginations. There are the imaginations that take place outside of our hearts, and the imaginations that stem from our hearts. Imaginations that take place outside our hearts are linked to external forces such as television, music, conversations and any communications we may have had voluntarily or involuntarily. Imaginations that stem from our hearts are things we have believed in, and things we have repeatedly subjected ourselves to, and these can include media, communications and associations as well. For example, if you listen to a song several times, it'll eventually get into your heart, and that's why people say, "I know the words by heart."

What many people don't know or understand is that we (human beings) are little gods.

Psalms 82:6: *I have said, Ye are gods; and all of you are children of the most High.*

John 10:34: *Jesus answered them, Is it not written in your law, I said, Ye are gods?*

As little gods, we are subject to the MOST HIGH GOD. We are made in HIS likeness, and we have many of HIS capabilities, although, on a much smaller scale, of course. JEHOVAH is our Creator; therefore, we are creatures. Because He created us in HIS likeness, we are creative, meaning, we have the ability to create most of what we imagine.

The purpose of our imaginations is not for us to entertain ourselves with sinful thoughts. The imagination is a waiting room and a window. It serves as a waiting room for thoughts, ideas, and anything that attempts to enter our hearts. We take what we already believe, and we measure it against whatever new information is being introduced to us. Within seconds, we decide whether we believe what's being communicated to us or if we don't believe it. If we believe it, we give it access to our hearts. If we don't believe it, we label it as false information, reject it and cast it out of our minds. When we reject new information, our minds automatically begin to label the person who brought us this information. For example, if you were to share this book with an unbeliever, and you mentioned that you love this book, the unbeliever would label you. You may be labeled as religious, brainwashed, crazy or misinformed. That's because we label what we do not understand, and we oftentimes give negative titles to people whose reports we don't believe. This helps us not to ponder on what was said, because we learn to reject what was said by reflecting on the label we've imposed on the person who said it.

Our imaginations also serve as a window. We get a chance to foresee what we want and what we do not want. We can place ourselves in situations that we have not yet entered. We can try a lifestyle on for size before deciding if we want that lifestyle, and before taking it to GOD in prayer. If we don't like what we've imagined, we continue shopping for new ideas. If we like what we've imagined, we continue to visit that imagination, and oftentimes, we communicate this information to Heaven, and ask that it be sent down to Earth for us. In other words, our imaginations are our fitting rooms, where we try on ideas to see if they fit us. People who don't pray a lot will oftentimes overwork themselves trying to accomplish what they've foreseen in their mind's eye.

Imaginations can be good, just as they can be evil. Anytime we imagine something that is not GOD'S will for us, our imaginations are considered evil, and we must cast them down. **2 Corinthians 10:5:** *Casting down imaginations, and every high thing that exalteth itself against the knowledge of God,* *and bringing into captivity every thought to the obedience of Christ.*

Why should we cast down or reject imaginations that exalt themselves against the knowledge of GOD? It's simple: Whatever we don't cast down, GOD will have to cast out of us. Any thought that steps into our mind's waiting room is a thought that should be compared with the WORD of GOD. When that thought isn't measured against the WORD, we'll end up spending too much time with that thought (meditation), thus, familiarizing ourselves with it. After an imagination has become familiar to us, we'll happily and easily allow it into our hearts.

Proverbs 4:23: *Keep thy heart with all diligence; for out of it are the issues of life.*

Whatever information we allow to enter into our hearts will begin to shape our perceptions, our lives and our realities. Because we are little gods, our worlds can be different from the worlds of our neighbors. Our worlds are our realities, and our realities are whatever we consider to be real. Realities and truth are not one and the same, even though most people link the two together. Our realities are whatever we have received as truth; they are whatever has manifested itself in our hearts, and oftentimes, before our eyes.

There's a reason, of course, that GOD told us to guard our hearts, and that reason is: Whatever we believe will eventually become our realities. It doesn't matter if what we believe is true or untrue. Whatever we allow to formulate in our minds will eventually come from our mouths and take life. Remember, we are little gods; therefore, we have life-changing capabilities in our minds and life-giving capabilities in our mouths. We can move mountains with our mouths, if we only have the faith to do so.

Proverbs 23:7: *For as he thinketh in his heart, so is he.*

Proverbs 18:20: *A man's belly shall be*

satisfied with the fruit of his mouth; and with the increase of his lips shall he be filled.
Mark 11:23: *For verily I say unto you, That whosoever shall say unto this mountain, Be thou removed, and be thou cast into the sea; and shall not doubt in his heart, but shall believe that those things which he saith shall come to pass; he shall have whatsoever he saith.*
Mark 11:24: *Therefore I say unto you, What things soever ye desire, when ye pray, believe that ye receive them, and ye shall have them.*

Have you ever noticed that people who see themselves as victims are always victimized? That's because we are whatever we believe ourselves to be. If we believe ourselves to be more than a conqueror through CHRIST JESUS, we will continue to overcome the obstacles that confront us. Our realities are not only shaped by our imaginations, our realities are shaped by our communications. Our communications aren't just with the people we exchange words with. Communications can also be one-way. Example: Someone communicates with us through music, movies and sermons. Some communications are exchanges of words between two or more people, and some communications are simply one person communicating with others. Whenever we are given a platform, we are given the opportunity to communicate with others without having to hear their opinions on the matter. When GOD told us to guard our hearts, HE wasn't just telling us to be careful who we give our hearts to; HE was telling us to be careful who we allow to have access to our minds, for whatever enters our minds will audition for a role in our hearts. Music is a great way for the enemy to enter into the hearts of billions of souls because, in music, the singer chants the same lyrics over and over again, helping the listeners to memorize what is said. Music is designed to help listeners remember the lyrics, and this is why it is one of Satan's favorite entryways. After a while, those lyrics don't have to ask for permission to enter our hearts, because we'll become familiar with them, and they'll slide right past our minds and enter directly into our hearts, whether we believe what's being said in the lyrics or not. That's why we rejoice when we hear a song we're familiar with. Our hearts can sing along, but in doing so, we stand in agreement with the singer.

Your mind is a doorway to your heart, and different thoughts, ideas, and words are always attempting to enter that doorway. You have to be careful who and what you allow to enter your mind, for whatever steps in you will eventually become a part of you. Every idea is attempting to mate with your mind and produce thoughts after itself. That's why GOD says that whatever a man thinks in his heart, so is he. Whatever a man believes will eventually become one with him, and begin to flow from him. This means that everything first introduces itself as an idea, and once it enters the mind, it becomes an imagination. If that imagination is not cast down, it enters the heart, and it becomes that person's heart issue or reality. Again, what a man believes does not have to be true in order for it to manifest itself in that man's life as his reality. Instead, when it begins to manifest, that person begins to live a lie. Think about a psychic, for example. Many psychics truly believe they are in communication with the dead, but, in truth, they are communicating with familiar spirits. These spirits have the ability to manifest themselves as the people we love. They are also able to manifest themselves in the forms of people we do not know and have never met. We must remember that these spirits (devils) have been around for thousands of years; therefore, they've met, influenced and even possessed many of our ancestors. To a psychic, these spirits are the spirits of the dead; therefore, their reality is that they communicate with dead people. It isn't true; however, but it's their reality, and it's real to them and the millions of people who trust in their powers. A person who trusts in the visions and beliefs of a psychic is also open to demonic visitation, attachment and sometimes possession.

If we want to live in the peace of GOD, and enjoy the blessings of GOD, we must first believe the WORD of GOD. A man who is sick will not have access to the healing power of GOD if he doesn't know or believe what the WORD says about his condition. If a man trusts more in a witch (psychic, sorcerer, diviner) than he does in the WORD of GOD, he will receive only that which a witch can offer him. If he receives healing from a witch, the truth is that he wasn't cured; the familiar spirits that infected him have simply taken a break so that he can continue to trust in them, and spread his beliefs to others. This helps them to grow their kingdom agenda. They've simply gone from actively attacking him to being dormant, but not by that witch's power; oftentimes, it's because of that man's influence with his family,

community or church. Devils want access to
more souls, so they use people to spread their
false doctrines.

Because we are little gods, we were given
dominion over our worlds (realities) by GOD,
but Satan wants to change our worlds. He
attempts to enter our hearts and present his
lies as imaginations and desires. If he is
granted access to our hearts, he begins to alter
our realities to fit his doctrine. Once our
realities have been altered by lies, we become
liars, also known as false teachers. We begin to
spread lies, worship lies and live lies. We also
begin to spread the wicked content of our
hearts to anyone who isn't rooted in the WORD
of GOD deep enough to know better. In other
words, we become ministers of darkness, and
we begin to evangelize for the kingdom of
darkness by spreading what we believe as
opposed to speaking the truth. You'll find
many cults in the realm of the earth today,
because some man or woman was visited by a

devil, and allowed that devil into his or her heart. They then began to passionately spread their lies. They became unyielding evangelists of Satan, and many of them are unaware of what they are spreading. Many times, Satan comes to people in the form of something or someone good, and this causes them to believe that they had a divine and Heavenly visitation by GOD or one of his angels, when, in truth, they were visited by the prince of darkness or one of his angels. For this reason, many people have learned to trust in witches (psychics, sorcerers, diviners) and every other dark power, but few trust in GOD.

2 Corinthians 11:13-15: *For such are false apostles, deceitful workers, transforming themselves into the apostles of Christ.*
And no marvel; for Satan himself is transformed into an angel of light. Therefore it is no great thing if his ministers also be transformed as the ministers of righteousness; whose end shall be according to their works.

Acts 16:16-18: *And it came to pass, as we*

went to prayer, a certain damsel possessed with a spirit of divination met us, which brought her masters much gain by soothsaying: The same followed Paul and us, and cried, saying, These men are the servants of the most high God, which shew unto us the way of salvation. And this did she many days. But Paul, being grieved, turned and said to the spirit, I command thee in the name of Jesus Christ to come out of her. And he came out the same hour.

Because whatever we believe becomes our realities, we have to be careful as to what thoughts we allow to sit in our hearts or entertain our minds. If we believe that we'll lose our homes to foreclosure, we will have what we believe ... and we'll lose our homes to foreclosure. If we believe that a disease will take us out of this world, rather than believing that the WORD of GOD has healed us, then a disease will take us out. Remember, we are very much like our FATHER who is in Heaven.

We have life-changing capabilities, just as we have life-giving capabilities. Our thoughts are powerless until they become our beliefs. Once a thought becomes a belief, it takes on the form of life, and it becomes our realities. Once it becomes our realities, it becomes an issue of ours, and it begins to flow from us to others.

How can we relate this truth to wealth, relationships and everything that stems from our lives? We do this by obeying the WORD of GOD, and believing what GOD says. We take the WORD and apply it to our lives, thus causing the WORD to become our realities, just as it is our truth. You see, when a man lives a lie, even though that lie is his reality, it's unstable, and will eventually fall; howbeit, the WORD of GOD will stand forever. If we take the WORD into our hearts, the WORD of GOD will begin to flow from our hearts and from our lives.

Whatever seeds we allow to enter our hearts

will eventually take root and grow up in our lives. If we want to change what we see manifesting before us, we have to change what we are allowing in us. There are many realities, opinions, and man-made ideas, but only the WORD of GOD shall stand against the tests of time.

Romans 3:4: *God forbid: yea, let God be true, but every man a liar; as it is written, That thou mightest be justified in thy sayings, and mightest overcome when thou art judged.*

Proverbs 19:21: *There are many devices in a man's heart; nevertheless the counsel of the LORD, that shall stand.*

Wealth Transfer & Reception

Lack is not the portion GOD set aside for the believer. Lack is an external state that represents the internal state of mind one has. Your mentality will always dress itself up as your reality and come to live with you. Needless to say, many believers live in lack because they have yet to renew their minds. Instead, most believers pack up their old mindsets and carry them into salvation with them. As a result, their lives don't change much because their minds haven't changed much. Many believers resort to charismatically chanting scriptures over and over again, hoping that they can call the blessings into the boxes they live in, when the blessings are calling them to step outside of their boxes.

Many churches today stray away from teaching

abundant living, and the ones who do teach it are often shunned and mislabeled as thieves. The truth is that there is a need for abundant living messages because CHRIST became poor so that we (the believer) could live in abundance. Many people shun such messages because they equate abundance with the love of wealth and material things, yet it's not one and the same. People often misquote 1 Timothy 6:10, which reads, *"For the love of money is the root of all evil: which while some coveted after, they have erred from the faith, and pierced themselves through with many sorrows."*

The misquoted version or "remix" of that scripture is "Money is the root of all evil" when, in truth, it is the <u>love of money</u> that is the root of all evil.

As 1 Timothy 6:10 warns us, many have coveted money, and this behavior has caused them to err from the faith. Truthfully, it's easy to covet after wealth when you see what wealth can do for you, but there is a reason that GOD told us to seek first the Kingdom of GOD and all its righteousness. In doing so, HE says that HE will add everything else to us. The reason we are told to seek the Kingdom of GOD is because anything we seek first becomes our master. It becomes the crown of our heads and the center of our lives. If we seek wealth before we seek the LORD, wealth will become our glory and our focus. We will then try to make GOD sit in the backseats of our hearts while we let the love of money drive us around. Additionally, a spirit called Mammon is directly associated with the love of money.

Matthew 6:24: *No man can serve two masters: for either he will hate the one, and love the other; or else he will hold to the one, and despise the other. Ye cannot serve God and mammon.*

Just how is wealth and lack transferred? How can we position ourselves to receive our portion of the wealth GOD avails to HIS children? Think about a bank account. In order for someone to transfer money into your bank account, you must first have a bank account. Our FATHER in Heaven is the Creator, Owner and Founder of this entire earth. Anytime we ask HIM for something that's in HIS will for us to have, HE initiates a transfer from Heaven to Earth with our names on it. But we can't access it if we don't have faith (our pin number). Our faith will allow us to receive the "yeas" and "amens" of GOD. Without faith, our blessings continue to dangle in the realm of the spirit. Additionally, anytime we ask GOD for something, GOD looks at the size of what we've asked for in comparison to our faith. Oftentimes, what we've asked for is a giant that dwarfs our faith; therefore, in order to give us what we've asked for, GOD first allows us to be tested and tried so that our faith can grow up. Faith won't grow unless it's fed or tested. We feed it by reading the WORD of GOD, meditating on the WORD of GOD and going to a GOD-ordained church. But when we don't get into the WORD as often as we should, tests often come along, and these tests are sometimes so big to us that we have no choice but to call on the Name of the LORD. It is then that we will seek HIS face. It is then that we will open our Bibles to search for answers. It is then that we will put away strife and fruitless bickering to concentrate on being restored. When we feel that we are under attack, we suddenly find the time to spend with the LORD. The goal is to get you to stop running from defeat to defeat and claim your victory through faith in CHRIST JESUS. It is to get your faith to grow up so big that it finally dwarfs the thing you've been praying for. Many times, we face situations that we perceive as giants, but anything that we see as "too much to bear" is an opportunity for GOD to show HIMSELF mighty, and to grow up our faith.

Next, we can only receive whatever amount we can believe GOD for. Many believe GOD for an eighty-thousand dollar house, but few believe

HIM for a million-dollar home. Because they have enough faith for an eighty-thousand dollar house, that's what they will receive. But when their faith grows up, and they can believe GOD for more, then they can receive more from GOD. It is the will of GOD to answer us with a yes, but we often tell ourselves "no" because we're accustomed to walking in the flesh, after the flesh and for the flesh. When your faith grows, your mind changes. Suddenly, you don't just want that million dollar home to lie around in and enjoy the high life. With grown up faith, you find yourself wanting that million dollar home because you want to glorify GOD with it. You want to show others what GOD can do for them, because HE did it for you. It becomes a part of your ministry, and not your lusts.

Wealth is linked to faith; whereas, lack is linked to fear. The Bible refers to Satan as a devourer who comes to steal, kill and destroy. One of the things that Satan comes to steal is our provision. He wants the believer to believe that there is no benefit to serving the LORD. Satan enriches many of the souls who serve him, but he doesn't do this because he loves them. Truthfully, we know that he hates them. He does this because they are vessels of darkness who are willing to mislead GOD'S people in exchange for riches and glory. At the same time, they exchange their very own souls for the wealth of this world. Satan wants to lead the sheep of GOD astray so that he can gather them in the wilderness of sin, where he intends to slaughter them with sickness, disease, poverty and lack of knowledge. He then intends to devour them.

Just how do wealth and lack transfer? Wealth transfers through faith; lack transfers through fear. But faith and fear stem from our belief systems, and what we receive is evidence of what we believe. What manifests for us will always be directly linked to whichever system we are tapped into, whether it be the system of faith or the system of fear.

Wealth is a state of mind that we have to be prepared for. Wealth does not come out to find us; we are invited into our wealthy places by GOD, but before we enter these sacred places, our minds go through a process of changing. We are shifted again and again until we find ourselves with a renewed mind. During this time, old friends walk away because we can no longer agree with them. Our minds have changed; therefore, our perceptions have changed, and even though our faces remain familiar to those who know us, our speech and choices become unrecognizable. When we are being prepared for our wealthy places, we'll often find ourselves heartbroken because of the people who are ripped out of our lives. New doors are opening, but not before the old ones close. As we are transferred from our familiar and comfortable lifestyles, we learn more about who we are in the LORD. That's when so many mysteries in our lives begin to unveil themselves, uncovering the answers to the questions that once eluded us. Wisdom becomes our garment, and she covers us like a beautiful wedding gown. She prepares us to enter into the blessings of GOD, where wealth, long life, health, and understanding await us like bridegrooms. That's when we begin to realize that wealth stayed still, but we had to be moved in order to reach it. Wealth is not a physical place; it is a state of mind that only few will enter, because we have to be dressed by wisdom in order to enter such a sacred place. It is dangerous to attain wealth without wisdom, for wisdom is your wealthy suit.

Think about a movie scene where an actor is separated from everyone he knows and loves and taken to a high-security place. He had to be kidnapped and taken to this place blindfolded because the kidnappers want to protect the location of their lairs. Once he arrives there, he is surprised to discover there is a whole new world out there; one he knew nothing of. That's how wealth works. Anytime we are shifted into our wealthy places, we are often taken there by surprise, with no one with us. After all, the journey is long, and many relationships fall by the wayside as we enter new realms; realms that many will never enter in their earthly life. It is then that we understand why we were separated from our loved ones, and blindfolded by our realities.

Your capacity to receive wealth is determined by wisdom. How far have you invited wisdom into your heart? After all, the heart is like soil, it has many depths to it, and when we believe something, it is either rooted deeply in our belief systems or it is easily unearthed. For example, religion is rooted deeply in the hearts of many people, and it's easier to pry a crying baby from its mother's arms than it is to pry religion from a strong man who swears by it. Wisdom has to be accepted into the innermost depths of your heart, and you must remain rooted in the WORD of GOD. When wisdom dwells in your heart, she will make room for every promise of GOD in your life. Wisdom's job is to prepare you for wealth; nevertheless, she is often rejected by man because of the sacrifices one must make to wear her. To be adorned with wisdom means we have to be stripped of our old mindsets and everything attached to those mindsets. It is to move into new realms of knowledge with no luggage or company, because every time we enter a new realm, we start off as infants in that realm until we've grown up. In each new realm, there is new understanding, new knowledge and wisdom dresses herself in new garments, and this can be intimidating for the average believer.

Lack, on the other hand, dresses itself in familiar garments. It pacifies our lusts and settles like dust around our minds. Lack is transferred through lack of knowledge, generational mindsets, associations and rebellion. Lack is oftentimes a comfortable place, because, as human beings, we learn to function wherever we are. Let's say one of your old friends was to see you in the supermarket one day, and the two of you start chatting. He sounds the same and his life hasn't really changed much. He's gotten older, but he's definitely not wiser. You feel this drawing of your soul. You want to hang out with him because you remember how funny he was and how much fun he was to be around. Your spirit man says that you should minister to him, but that old flesh of yours wants to go back and relive the past. What's happening is you're being pulled on by familiarity. You feel relaxed around what you know, but GOD is taking you into realms of the unknown, and this is an uncomfortable place. If you go back and rekindle the relationship with that old friend, you are rekindling your relationship with whatever it was that linked the two of you—and that includes lack. You see, GOD won't bring you into your wealthy place until you've released all of the people HE'S forbidden in your life. You can't enter your wealthy place if you're in disobedience. The realm of rebellion is a bottomless pit where sinners descend into darkness; howbeit, wealth is a strong tower built by GOD, and anyone who reaches it must ascend in CHRIST to reach it.

How does one attract wealth to himself? Again, we attract what we are. When we are a blessing, we attract blessings. When we serve as stumbling blocks for others, we attract stumbling blocks. Wealth is attracted to wisdom; therefore, if you'd like to receive abundance, you must first seek wisdom and be prepared to go the full distance of wherever she leads you. You can't faint when the journey takes you through the wilderness. The purpose of going through the wilderness is to get you out of a mindset that you have. At the same time, GOD doesn't enrich us for us; HE enriches us for HIS people as a whole. HE enriches us to show others what HE can do for them. HE enriches HIS children to provide us with the ability to be random blessings to others. So, if you want to receive the blessings of GOD, you have to be a blessing of GOD.

Confessions, Declarations & Decrees

What is a confession, declaration and a decree? The following definitions are from merriam-webster.com.

Confession:

- a written or spoken statement in which you say that you have done something wrong or committed a crime
- the act of telling people something that makes you embarrassed, ashamed, etc.
- the act of telling your sins to God or to a priest

Declaration:

- the act of making an official statement about something: the act of declaring something
- something that is stated or made known in an official or public way

- a document that contains an official statement: a document that makes a declaration

Decree:

- an official order given by a person with power or by a government
- an official decision made by a court of law

The Bible tells us to confess our sins one to another. To confess is to admit one's guilt. It is to admit that GOD is right by acknowledging that you are wrong. Anytime we confess a thing, we serve it eviction papers from our hearts. We are saying to those old ways that we no longer want them to be a part of us. In this, we are transferring our burdens to the LORD, for those burdens serve as yokes about our necks.

One of the reasons GOD calls us to confess our sins is to get us to acknowledge that they are wrong. Anytime we don't acknowledge that something is wrong, we learn to rationalize it and live with it. Once we acknowledge that it's wrong, it steps outside of our hearts, and we are given another chance to change our minds. To confess your sins is to humble yourself before GOD.

James 5:16: *Confess your faults one to another, and pray one for another, that ye may be healed. The effectual fervent prayer of a righteous man availeth much.*

1 John 1:9: *If we confess our sins, he is faithful and just to forgive us our sins, and to cleanse us from all unrighteousness.*

2 Chronicles 7:14: *If my people, which are called by my name, shall humble themselves, and pray, and seek my face, and turn from their wicked ways; then will I hear from heaven, and will forgive their sin, and will heal their land.*

To declare a thing is to announce it publicly after first having accepted it as truth in your own heart. Any person can go out and say something they don't believe, but in doing so, they didn't make a declaration; they simply told a lie. To declare a thing is to make it official in your life.

GOD said that if we declared a thing, it would be so. Needless to say, many of us have said many things, and we have yet to see the manifestation of our words. Why is this? It's simple. Again, in order for a declaration to be a declaration, we must first believe it ourselves. Many people say what they want, but they have yet to attach faith to their words. A declaration is words set in motion by faith. It is to boldly and publicly announce what you already believe.

Why are declarations important to GOD? Because declaring a thing is what makes us like HIM. When GOD said, "Let there be light," we know that light immediately existed. Everything GOD declares is so, and that's why it is impossible for GOD to tell a lie. Anything GOD has spoken immediately and automatically begins to exist the very second HE speaks it. When we make a declaration, we are setting our faith in motion. It's one thing to have faith, but we too must have the works or evidence of our faith. Additionally, to declare something is to send out words that agree with GOD against words and mindsets that are against HIM. A declaration is a bold statement; one in which the speaker displays their unmovable faith.

Luke 1:2-2: *Forasmuch as many have taken in hand to set forth in order a declaration of those things which are most surely believed among us, even as they delivered them unto us, which from the beginning were eyewitnesses, and ministers of the word.*

To make a decree is to establish something as law in your life and home. One cannot make a declaration without a decree, for a declaration takes place on the outside; whereas, a decree must first become official in our hearts before we are able to make it law in our lives. When we decree something, it no longer becomes a possibility; it becomes our reality. To decree a thing is to pull it from the inside and cause it to take form or exist on the outside.

Job 22:28: *Thou shalt also decree a thing, and it shall be established unto thee: and the light shall shine upon thy ways.*

In order to receive something from GOD, we must give up something. Oftentimes, we are required to renounce mindsets and lies so that we can have the capacity to receive a renewed mind and truth. Truth and lies cannot dwell together, just as darkness and light cannot coexist. Therefore, to receive something from GOD, we must empty ourselves out. We bring our ways, thoughts and confusions to HIM, and in return, HE gives us HIS ways, HIS knowledge and peace of mind. In other words, HE gives us the capacity to receive what we've been praying for. HE gives us a slice of Heaven. Reception never takes place until a transfer has been made. Think about a satellite dish. It is nothing more than a metal dish if there are no signals for it to receive. In order for a satellite to work, a signal must first be sent out or transferred. Once that signal is transferred, the satellite will receive it if the satellite is in the signal's range. As believers, we are similar to satellite dishes. We have to be in GOD'S will (range) for us to receive the transmissions that GOD has already sent to us. Oftentimes, people are not in position, but are somewhere in false doctrines, sin and perverse mindsets trying to pick up a signal from Heaven. It is not uncommon to find a saint sitting in rebellion attempting to make declarations with no inner decrees. It is not uncommon to find a believer in sin trying to pull down an inheritance with their mouths, while sitting outside of their FATHER'S will. In order to receive our portion of the will of GOD, we must get in GOD'S will for our lives. We do this by obeying GOD, not just with our actions, but with our hearts. We must first agree with GOD in order to obey HIM, and when we agree with HIM, our lives will decree our faith before our mouths declare it.

Anytime you confess a thing, you empty yourself out to receive GOD'S blessings. The more you empty yourself out of sin, the more you will and can receive from GOD.
Anytime you declare a thing, you speak to the masses what your heart has decreed. It has to be law in your life before you can teach it to others. That's why the LORD told us to remove the plank from our own eyes before attempting to remove it from someone else's. Anytime we are changed by GOD, we receive the power to change others through our decrees, testimonies, declarations and confessions.
After all, when our mouths speak a thing that our lives don't reflect, we are labeled hypocrites, and our ministries become nothing more than religious entertainment with no power.

Doors & Windows

John 10:1: *Verily, verily, I say unto you, He that entereth not by the door into the sheepfold, but climbeth up some other way, the same is a thief and a robber.*

Our behaviors, thoughts and plans are either legal or illegal with GOD. Oftentimes, it's relatively easy to discern what's inside of the gray lines of righteousness, and what's outside. Anytime we are driven or led by our flesh, chances are, we are outside of GOD'S will. Anytime we are led by our spirit man, we are inside of GOD'S will. This is because our spirit man (after salvation) is quickened and made alive by the HOLY SPIRIT of GOD. Our flesh, on the other hand, remains the same; lusting after unholy things. For this reason, it is easy for us to fall into sin, even after being saved, and that's why GOD warns us not to be led of our flesh.

The flesh has a system that it's accustomed to, and it signals our minds to feed into this system. Whenever we give the flesh what it wants, it signals back to us that we have satisfied it. When we don't give in to the desires of the flesh, it often protests by consuming our thoughts and causing lust to rise up in our mortal bodies. For example, if you've decided that you are going to eat healthy foods when your flesh is accustomed to junk food, you may experience adverse reactions. You may experience headaches, nausea, slothfulness, and sometimes break-outs. That's because your flesh has its own system, and it demands that this system is followed. But when you go against the flesh repeatedly, it begins to submit to your spirit man, and you learn to walk after your spirit and not your flesh.

The flesh will always take you through the window (illegal behaviors) and not the door (legal behaviors). That's because the flesh is impatient and wants what it wants when it wants it. With GOD, we have to be patient; therefore, the flesh and the spirit are in opposition of one another at all times. For this reason, obesity is a problem in this earth, since many people go after "fast food" rather than taking the time to prepare a healthy meal. Because many are impatient, fornication is on the rise, since many people refuse to wait on GOD for the spouses HE has for them. Being overly anxious is one of the traits of the flesh; whereas, patience is a fruit of the SPIRIT.

Galatians 5:16-24: *This I say then, Walk in the Spirit, and ye shall not fulfil the lust of the flesh. For the flesh lusteth against the Spirit, and the Spirit against the flesh: and these are contrary the one to the other: so that ye cannot do the things that ye would. But if ye be led of the Spirit, ye are not under the law. Now the works of the flesh are manifest, which* *are these; Adultery, fornication, uncleanness, lasciviousness, idolatry, witchcraft, hatred, variance, emulations, wrath, strife, seditions, heresies, envyings, murders, drunkenness, revellings, and such like: of the which I tell you before, as I have also told you in time past, that they which do such things shall not inherit the kingdom of God. But the fruit of the Spirit is love, joy, peace, longsuffering, gentleness, goodness, faith, meekness, temperance: against such there is no law. And they that are Christ's have crucified the flesh with the affections and lusts.*

In Galatians 5:16-24, we are taught just how different the flesh and the spirit are. One desires to do the opposite of what the other desires. The flesh is accustomed to being in the lead. After all, when we were children, we were taught to feed and nurture our flesh. Our parents nurtured our flesh and helped many of us to develop the systems we follow today. They bathed, fed and groomed our flesh, and because of this, our flesh began to grow. As the flesh grew stronger, it began to dwarf our spirit man. Once we got saved, we found ourselves with an assignment that would span across many years. That assignment was to learn to feed our spirit by reading the WORD of GOD, and applying HIS WORD to our lives. Sunday morning service isn't enough, because we've been climbing into windows most of our lives, and now, we're being told to use the doors. That is, we are being taught to follow the lead of GOD, as opposed to following the system of our flesh.

Whatever you feed will grow, and whatever you starve will weaken and eventually die. Anytime we feed our flesh, our flesh grows stronger, but anytime we feed our spirit man, our flesh grows weaker as our spirit becomes stronger. The desires of the flesh lead to death; therefore, we should not appease the flesh. Instead, we ought to starve it. Now, does this mean that we are to stop eating altogether? Of course not. To starve the flesh, as it relates to GOD, is to not give in to its desires. It is to oppose the system of the flesh in order to appease the LORD. When you want to see a move of GOD, you must first be still. When you want GOD to hear you, you must first speak. When you want GOD to speak, you must first be silent. Everything you do with GOD requires faith. If you think that you must speak many words for GOD to hear you, you miss out on the opportunity to let GOD speak to you. If you think you need to do many works for GOD to move, you miss out on the opportunity of seeing GOD move in your situation. GOD will not share HIS glory, so if we want HIM to take the lead, we must first learn to follow HIM.

Our flesh is always trying to lead the LORD, just as it tries to lead us. For this reason, you'll find many believers attempting to change the WORD of GOD to pacify the all-too-consuming desires of their unquenchable flesh. But to get the laws of Heaven and Earth to work in our favor, we must first understand that GOD will not be mocked. To be mocked is to be imitated. To be mocked also means to be ridiculed. People often attempt to imitate GOD by telling themselves and others what they feel is allowable, even when what they feel is not scriptural. People often ridicule GOD by ridiculing HIS WORD when they don't agree with it. Many people throw stones at GOD'S Messengers when they don't like the messages. Some people throw physical stones, while others throw hard words at anyone delivering a WORD from GOD that is not welcomed in their hearts. That's because many people don't understand that GOD is HIS WORD, and by rejecting HIS WORD, they, in turn, reject HIM. Many would-be believers go to the sanctuary and perform religious acts of worship after having rejected the Truth. That's because many people serve the false image of GOD that they have erected in their hearts, and, therefore, do not know the one and only true and living GOD, YAHWEH (JEHOVAH). It's easy to create an image in our minds and begin to worship that image, but in order for us to worship JEHOVAH (YAHWEH), we must worship HIM in Spirit and in Truth. Any other forms of worship do not rise up to HIM; instead, they become nothing more than harmonized noise.

To get the law of transfer to work in our favor, we must know the WORD of GOD, agree with the WORD of GOD, and obey HIM. Many people know and obey the scriptures through performance, rather than by obeying GOD in love. The difference is, when we know and understand what GOD says, and why HE says it, we are able to agree with GOD and make HIS command a part of our will. If we perform an act that we don't want to perform, it becomes more like forced labor, and GOD does not want us to take this mindset with HIM.

2 Corinthians 9:7: *Every man according as he purposeth in his heart, so let him give; not grudgingly, or of necessity: for God loveth a cheerful giver.*

When we learn to oppose our flesh and walk after the spirit, we learn to patiently await the seasons that GOD has set in motion for our lives. When we walk after the flesh, we attempt to enter into those seasons illegally, because of impatience, envy, the desire to boast, and so on. When we willfully and joyfully serve GOD with our lives and choices, the blessings of GOD manifest outwardly to represent the fruit of the SPIRIT that has blossomed inwardly. Needless to say, when we are disobedient, we tap into the already declared WORD of GOD as it relates to a son or daughter in rebellion. In rebellion, a son forfeits his inheritance because he no longer walks as a son, but as one who opposes his father. Please understand that the WORD of GOD has already been declared, and it will not return to HIM void. HIS WORD does not change to give us more space to enjoy the perks of living a flesh-filled life. Instead, if we want to tap into the blessings of GOD, we must continue to walk as sons and daughters of GOD. Sure, HIS grace covers us, but HIS WORD continues to declare itself as Truth, whether we stay in HIS will or step outside of HIS will. Consider the parable that CHRIST spoke about the prodigal son. *(See Luke 15:11-32).* The prodigal son asked his father for his inheritance, and then went away to a far-away land and squandered his inheritance. Suddenly, a famine arose in that land, and being outside of his father's house, the prodigal son ended up working for someone as a servant; nevertheless, he was still starving. Finally, he decided to go back to his father's house and acknowledge (confession) that he'd committed evil against his father (repentance). Once he was back in his father's house, his father threw a feast for him, and he was able to live the life of a son, instead of a famished servant in a foreign land. Such is the ways of mankind and GOD. When we take what GOD gives us and run off into sin, we live outside of GOD'S will, and we have to endure the famines and the hardships of the world we serve. We become foreigners in a world that hates us, but loves what we have to offer. But once we get back in the will of GOD, first having confessed our sins and then having repented of our sins, we can go back to living as sons and daughters of the Most High GOD.

Have you ever heard someone speak of another person having open doors in their lives that the enemy uses to come in and out of their lives? Have you ever heard it prophesied over someone that GOD is opening doors in their lives? Doors represent levels in the realm of the spirit. When a demonic access door is open, it often represents an area of a person's heart that is not guarded. For example, you may meet a woman who refrains from fornication, but is still an active gambler. Gambling is an access door in her life, and this door gives devils access to her finances and her mind. Or there may be a man who goes out and ministers to the masses, yet, he continues to commit adultery against his wife. Adultery is an open door that allows the enemy to come in and attack his marriage, his mind and his health. How so? Any sin committed with the body is a sin committed against the body. Additionally, any sin committed against his wife is a sin committed against his marriage. You'll find that wherever someone has an opened door, it is in that area of their life that they are often led astray and attacked. At the same time, it is that area of their life wherein they have learned to communicate with and depend on the devil; whether they say his name or not. Think about the gambling woman. Gamblers usually have problems with their finances. There are windows open in their finances that the enemy uses to rob them. Remember, Satan is more than a liar; he is a thief, and he's always looking to steal something. Because she is a gambler, she is likely tuned into fortune-telling, horoscopes and other dark powers. That's because gamblers often believe in "chance" as opposed to believing the WORD of GOD. Because she doesn't believe HIM, she has learned to believe in other powers. Therefore, as a gambler, that woman taps into the demonic realm looking for the abundance that CHRIST has already provisioned for the believer. In tapping into chance, luck and fortune-telling, she is tapping into familiar spirits. Think about the man in adultery. Arguments are likely commonplace in his home. Additionally, he lives in fear of his wife discovering his infidelities; therefore, he's always having to commune with lying spirits for new stories to tell his wife and his mistress. In other words, because these people did not wait for GOD to open new doors and new understandings in their lives, they went through windows looking for blessings in sin. The blessings of GOD remain in HIS will, and we must be in HIS will to inherit them; otherwise, we go into foreign places and squander our inheritance.

Faith vs Fear

Hebrews 11:1: *Now faith is the substance of things hoped for, the evidence of things not seen.*

2 Timothy 1:7: *For God hath not given us the spirit of fear; but of power, and of love, and of a sound mind.*

2 Corinthians 4:13: *We having the same spirit of faith, according as it is written, I believed, and therefore have I spoken; we also believe, and therefore speak.*

In reading the WORD of GOD, you will notice that GOD often contrasts right decisions with wrong decisions. HE tells us what to expect when we trust and obey HIM, and what to expect when we don't trust or obey HIM. In reading 2 Timothy 1:7, we see that HE contrasts fear with power. We can either have fear or we can have power, but we can't have both. At the same time, HE contrasts fear with love and with a sound mind. This means that we can't love what we fear, nor can we have peace in the midst of fear, for the two oppose one another. We can love and fear the LORD, however, because GOD is love. To fear GOD is to acknowledge that we have faith in HIM; therefore, just as we believe HE can bless and heal us, we also believe that HE can punish us greatly. To fear HIM is to acknowledge HIS power.

We are vessels; we know this. But what many people don't know or understand is that a vessel is designed to carry cargo. Our cargo is what we believe. Either we are carrying around the WORD of GOD, or we are carrying around false doctrine and the burdens of our flesh. Additionally, whatever we are carrying determines our destinations, and not just our forever homes; our cargo determines where we are headed in the realm of the earth. After all, you can't take foolishness to a wise man or he will reject it, just as you can't take wisdom to a foolish man or he will hate you. So, if you are filled with wisdom, you will go before great men and women to deliver what GOD has stored up in you. GOD ships wisdom to the Kingdom-minded; therefore, if you want to go into Kingdom-like places, you must first be a vessel full of wisdom. If you are foolish, you will go alongside or behind foolish men as they plan, plot and scheme their way through life. Whatever is stored up in you is the very thing that has set the GPS on your life and has taken you to where you are, and will continue to take you to souls like yourself to deliver whatever is in you. Therefore, if we want to get the blessings of GOD, we have to become a blessing for GOD. If we want to be carriers of wisdom, we must set ourselves in a position to receive the wisdom. Additionally, we have to be faithful vessels, delivering what GOD has stored up in us to HIS people. All too often, many believers take what GOD has given them and begin to consume it. They don't share with their brethren; instead, they shower it upon themselves. For this reason, GOD often tests us by giving us a little so we can understand why HE is not giving us a lot at that time. HE knows whether we are faithful or not. After all, HE sees our hearts. Many of the tests that fall upon us are designed to help us see what GOD already sees. Whenever we become faithful vessels of God, HE rewards our faithfulness by giving us access to HIS "yea" and "amens".

Proverbs 9:8-9: *Reprove not a scorner, lest he hate thee: rebuke a wise man, and he will love thee. Give instruction to a wise man, and he will be yet wiser: teach a just man, and he will increase in learning.*

Proverbs 17:10: *A reproof enters more into a wise man than a hundred stripes into a fool.*

James 4:3: *Ye ask, and receive not, because ye ask amiss, that ye may consume it upon your lusts.*

Matthew 25:21: *His lord said unto him, Well done, thou good and faithful servant: thou hast*

been faithful over a few things, I will make thee
ruler over many things: enter thou into the joy
of thy lord.

Faith and fear operate by the same law. Faith is
reverencing GOD and believing the WORD of
God; whereas, fear stems from believing
Satan's report. Fear is having faith in the devil.
Anytime we fear something, we revere that
thing and agree with its report. Anytime we
have faith in GOD, we revere GOD and agree
with HIS WORD.
But how can we obtain more faith, thus
allowing ourselves to become glowing vessels
of GOD sent out to deliver the good news to
GOD'S people? It's simple. By storing up the
wisdom GOD has set out for HIS children to
partake of.

One of the most effective strategies of Satan is
to get believers to minimize the value of
wisdom. Satan knows what wisdom brings.
Wisdom brings health, wealth, knowledge,

understanding and long life. The enemy's plan is to get believers to focus on the things in the realm of the earth, because he understands that a distracted believer is just as ineffective as an unbeliever. A wise believer, on the other hand, is a person who will radiate and demonstrate GOD'S blessings to believers and unbelievers alike. So, to get believers to take their eyes off GOD (in faith), the enemy looks for voids in their lives. He looks for open doors in their hearts and homes; doors in which he intends to enter and attack. Just like a snake, he delivers his venom (fear), and it paralyzes anyone who is infected by it. And just like a snake, he begins to devour his prey once it is paralyzed. Faith is anti-venom, and the enemy is afraid of a believer who is full of faith.

Whatever we store in our hearts, it is that which we will receive. Everything that manifests outwardly in our lives comes forth to represent what's going on in our hearts. Additionally, anytime we become vessels of faith, we begin to store up the very blessings we are being used to deliver to others. Sure, the storms may come and beat upon our sails, but most storms are there to get us to cast out whatever Jonah we have aboard our vessels. Our Jonahs can be family members, romantic interests, jobs, friends or poisoned mindsets. Additionally, we can be our own Jonahs if we are attempting to flee from our GOD-given assignments.

Faith comes to add to us; fear comes to subtract from us. All the same, we become like the people we hang out with because, like us, they too are vessels transferring whatever doctrines they have in their hearts.
Proverbs 13:20: *He that walketh with wise men shall be wise: but a companion of fools shall be destroyed.*

Friction vs Harmony

What exactly is friction, and what is harmony? The following definitions were taken from Google.

Friction:

- the resistance that one surface or object encounters when moving over another.
- the action of one surface or object rubbing against another.
- conflict or animosity caused by a clash of wills, temperaments, or opinions.

Harmony:

- the combination of simultaneously sounded musical notes to produce chords and chord progressions having a pleasing effect.
- agreement or concord.

Let's start first with friction, and how it relates

to our lives. We've all experienced friction with other human beings, and most of the time when we do experience friction, we experience it with those closest to us. That's because an object has to rub against or strike another object before friction can take place. Friction happens when two or more objects oppose one another, just as it occurs when two or more people oppose one another.

One thing you'll notice about friction is that it oftentimes causes a surge of power or electricity. In many cases, when two objects oppose one another directly, one or both of those objects will store electricity or heat for a short period of time. For example, if two vehicles were to strike one another, the impact from both vehicles would cause each vehicle's area of impact to become warm to the touch.

There are two kinds of friction noted in physics. They are static friction and kinetic friction. The following definitions are courtesy of Google.

Static Friction: Friction between two or more solid objects that are not moving relative to each other.

Kinetic Friction: Between two hard surfaces, the kinetic friction is usually somewhat lower than the static friction, meaning that more force is required to set the objects in motion than to keep them in motion.

When we are dealing with other human beings, we are either moving with them or against them. Anytime we move with someone, we are in agreement. Anytime we move against someone, we cause friction.

Amos 3:3: *Can two walk together, except they be agreed?*

In our relationships with other human beings, we come to understand just how we, as individuals, deal with friction. What happens when our friends don't agree with us? Can we stay in a relationship with someone who is heading in the opposite direction? The WORD of GOD answers these questions for us. Again, Amos 3:3 asks the question, "Can two walk together, except they be agreed?" In other words, the author is asking, "How can two people walk together if they are not in agreement with one another?" The simple answer is: They can't. Sure, we won't always agree with one another, but opinions are usually not rooted deep enough to cause us to separate from our loved ones, even though varying opinions do cause friction. What usually separates families, friends and marriages are those beliefs that are deeply rooted in each individual person. Beliefs such as religious and political beliefs are oftentimes rooted deep enough to separate the strongest of bonds. Why is that? Think about two small metal objects striking up against one another. Sure, sparks will oftentimes fly if enough force is exerted from each object, but there's usually not enough power there to cause a fire. But if two large objects traveling at a high rate of speed were to strike each other (depending on the weight and speed of each object), in many cases, enough force is exerted to cause a fire. Many of our beliefs work in a similar manner. We are all driven by what we believe, and the more rooted a belief is in us, the more power that belief has to us. Anytime someone opposes something that is deeply rooted within us, it usually has enough impact to separate us from that person. For example, if your best friend doesn't agree with you about which basketball team is the greatest of all time, it wouldn't be a big deal to you because basketball is just a game. It does not shape your life unless you are a professional basketball player or a coach. If basketball is not paying your bills, any opinions expressed will likely not have enough power to separate you from the person expressing their opinion. Needless to say, however, if someone were to say that they are Republican and don't agree with the Democratic agenda, and you happen to be Democratic; oftentimes, this would be enough to separate you from them. The reason is, many people center their lives around politics; whereas, most people don't center their lives around sports.

When two or more people unify and attempt to travel this journey we call life together, they have to be in agreement as to what destination they are attempting to reach. Additionally, they must agree on the direction in which they plan to travel to get there. When two or more people attempt to merge their lives as friends or as a couple, friction ensues if each individual is not headed in the same direction as their partner. Instead of working together, each force begins to oppose one another, and this is called opposition. Opposition is the opposing of one's position. In marriages, such friction can exert enough force to cause the husband and wife to violently oppose one another in a final act of desperation called divorce.

Malachi 2:16: *The man who hates and divorces his wife," says the LORD, the God of Israel, "does violence to the one he should* *protect," says the LORD Almighty. So be on your guard, and do not be unfaithful.*

Because we must agree in order to walk together, GOD specifically commanded that we not be unequally yoked with unbelievers. A believer and an unbeliever may look similar, but they are not the same. The direction of an unbeliever is towards eternal damnation, and unbelievers are led by their flesh, just as they are oftentimes led by demonic spirits. Believers, on the other hand, are traveling the road of righteousness, and are led by the HOLY SPIRIT of GOD. Anytime a believer and an unbeliever intermarry, friction will ensue unless one of the spouses is to turn and follow the other spouse. Just as our beliefs in GOD are deeply rooted, an unbeliever's beliefs are oftentimes even more deeply rooted because they've learned to walk after their flesh all of their lives. Whatever force has been leading them is now a familiar force to them; therefore, to abandon what they know is like abandoning who they are. It takes GOD to reach in and turn our hearts around. Anytime two people walk together in unity, the force behind those two is greater than the forces that oppose them, and this is why Satan fights marriage with such fury. A husband and wife walking together as one person is too powerful for Satan and his whole kingdom of devils to oppose. Two believing friends who love and fear the LORD, and are called according to HIS purpose, can exert enough power to rid a whole city of devils. So, to save himself and his kingdom, Satan oftentimes perverts our beliefs so that we can operate against one another.

If a car were to hit a wall, depending on the rate of speed and the weight of the car, that wall may come tumbling down. If the wall is built with sturdy materials, and the car that impacted it was to hit it at a low rate of speed, the car may sustain damage; whereas, the wall may not. This is to say that a moving object can cause enough friction to bring down another object that is not moving. Think of how that relates to us as believers. If a believer is not rooted in the WORD of GOD, and someone was to challenge their beliefs, the unbeliever may have enough power to move the believer. That's because there wasn't enough WORD in the believer to steady them. That's why you'll find many unstable believers who sample ungodly doctrines and try to incorporate those beliefs into their lives. But if an unbeliever were to challenge a believer who is firmly rooted and unmovable in the WORD of GOD, the only person moved or damaged by the force exerted in the impact would be the unbeliever. That's why GOD tells us not to argue with a fool. The WORD has enough power in it to stand against any force that opposes it; therefore, all we have to do is stand on the WORD and let the LORD speak for HIMSELF.

Anytime two objects oppose one another, some of the energy used to move each object will transfer into the objects opposing it. Of course, we know this energy as friction. People often store up positive and negative energy, and those who walk with us oftentimes transfer their positive energy to us. That's why you'll notice that a positive friend will oftentimes lift your spirit with just a few words, but a negative person will drain you without saying a word. Negative people draw energy from others, and anytime their negative energy is met with positive energy, they often become agitated. That's because negative energy opposes all that is positive. Negative people love to be around negative people because they are walking in agreement with one another. If you have a negative friend, try being positive every time they call. If they start gossiping about someone, tell them to pray for that person. If they complain about the traffic, tell them they are blessed to have a vehicle. If they complain about their vehicle, tell them to bless someone else with that vehicle. Anytime you meet negative energy with positive energy, opposition will ensue, and friction will manifest itself.

Have you ever noticed that when someone is agitated, they oftentimes want to agitate everyone around them? Let's say that you are married, for example. Your spouse comes home and slams the door. He or she begins to storm through the house, mumbling and complaining about their job. You intercept them in the kitchen and try to offer them some of the iced tea that you are drinking. What's likely to happen? They'll sharply rebuke you or vehemently reject your iced tea. After that, they'll likely tell you about the tone of their day. In many cases, a spouse will accuse you of wrongdoing or remind you of something you did wrong. That's because they need to walk "with" you, and the two of you cannot walk together unless you are in agreement with one another. This means they need you to be in the same spirit they are in, and it's easy to get a person into their flesh by simply opposing them. In order to overcome the spirit of strife that has invaded your home, you would have to literally love the hell out of your spouse. Fury in a person is nothing more than spiritual heartburn from chewing on a slice of hell. You have to oppose evil with good, and this isn't always easy; especially, when the infuriated person wants to remain in their fury.

Romans 12:21: *Be not overcome of evil, but overcome evil with good.*

Whatever energy is stored up in a person is exerted by whatever beliefs that person has in their hearts. The deeper that belief is rooted, the more force behind it. Additionally, two people who are not in agreement cannot walk together; therefore, anytime they attempt to merge their lives, friction will arise between them until they are finally worn thin or change directions. Finally, any person not grounded by the WORD can be easily moved when someone whose beliefs are more rooted than theirs opposes their beliefs.

What about harmony? Again, Google defines harmony as:

- the combination of simultaneously sounded musical notes to produce chords and chord progressions having a pleasing effect.
- agreement or concord.

In musical terms, harmony is a pleasant sound that arises when musical notes are sounded simultaneously. In non-musical terms, harmony is when two or more people are in agreement or walk in one accord. With GOD, harmony is the beautiful sound and sight of HIS people walking together as one in HIM for HIS glory. When two or more people walk together in one accord, they become even more powerful than they were as one person. Think about the natural realm. If one man were to try and lift a fifty-pound box, he'd have to use more of his muscles than he would if he lifted a twenty-pound box. If another man were to assist him in lifting the box, both men would find that the box feels lighter because the weight of the box is being shared.

The same occurs when we walk together in unity for the sake of the Kingdom. Any problem that attacks a believer comes with only as much force as that believer gives it. For example, if someone fears losing their home to foreclosure, the force that's opposing them is fear. But if that person had a believing friend to intercede on their behalf, their friend's faith may be greater than their fears. Because faith is a positive force, it is a stronger force than fear; therefore, the home would not be lost. This is why GOD calls us to walk in unity, and confess our sins one to the other.

Genesis 11:6: *And the LORD said, Behold, the people is one, and they have all one language; and this they begin to do: and now nothing will be restrained from them, which they have imagined to do.*

Hebrews 10:25: *Not forsaking the assembling of ourselves together, as the manner of some is; but exhorting one another: and so much the* *more, as ye see the day approaching.*

When two or more people are unmovable in their faith, and those people walk together in the LORD, they walk in harmony. Each step in the LORD that they make together sounds as Heavenly as a well-harmonized choir singing praises to GOD. Every step that believers take together in agreement is a step that the enemy cannot oppose. Satan has absolutely no power against unity; therefore, Satan specializes in friction and division.

You'll notice that whenever you have a believing friend, the enemy is always magnifying their imperfections to you. Let's face it: We are all imperfect beings. We've learned to live with our own imperfections, so much so that we oftentimes don't notice them, but when we see our friends' imperfections, they stand out to us. For example, let's say you have a friend who happens to have a bit of a temper. This friend is GOD-fearing, and you know that GOD is with them, but you've also seen their flesh in action. You saw them lose their temper with a woman at the park who'd yelled at them over a parking spot. You were there to hold your friend back as she attempted to advance towards the woman who was opposing her. You saw this friend lose her temper with a few members of her family, and she was the aggressor. You've seen your friend argue back and forth with a police officer who had ticketed her for parking without a permit. You've seen your friend's flesh, and because of this, your perception of her is in danger of changing. Now you are questioning her relationship with GOD altogether, not understanding that every man or woman wrapped in flesh has imperfections. David loved women so much that he took Uriah's wife (Bathsheba), and set Uriah in front of a war so that he'd be killed. Samson loved women so much that he went against Jewish tradition and married Delilah, a Phoenician. Simon Peter cut off the servant of the high priest's ear. Paul used to be Saul, and he'd murdered, intimidated and threatened many of the disciples of GOD. Abraham lied and said that Sarah was his sister, when in truth, she was his wife. Every man of GOD in the Bible had imperfections, just as we are imperfect.

Can you still trust and respect your friend knowing that she has a temper, or would her temper change your perception of her? The enemy shows us the imperfections of our friends so that we can no longer walk in harmony with them. Instead, we tend to focus on everything that's wrong with that friend so intently that we lose focus of everything that's right with that friend. In other words, we stop walking in harmony with them when we start to watch their steps and not our own.

Matthew 7:1-5: *Judge not, that ye be not judged. For with what judgment ye judge, ye shall be judged: and with what measure ye mete, it shall be measured to you again. And why beholdest thou the mote that is in thy brother's eye, but considerest not the beam* *that is in thine own eye? Or how wilt thou say to thy brother, Let me pull out the mote out of thine eye; and, behold, a beam is in thine own eye? Thou hypocrite, first cast out the beam out of thine own eye; and then shalt thou see clearly to cast out the mote out of thy brother's eye.*

Noah was imperfect. One night, he'd gotten drunk and fell asleep naked in his tent. Ham, who was one of his sons, saw his drunk, naked and exposed father. Instead of covering his father, he told his brothers what he'd seen. In the text, it's easy to see that Ham exposed his father. Noah's other two sons, Shem and Japheth, walked in backwards so they wouldn't see their father naked, and they covered him up. The Bible goes on to tell us that Noah blessed Shem and Japheth for what they'd done, but he cursed Ham. Noah was by all means imperfect, but he was still a man of GOD. If GOD had not favored him, Noah would have died in the flood, but GOD forewarned him, and gave him the provision he needed to build the ark and save himself and his family. Nevertheless, Noah was still imperfect.

You are still imperfect no matter how hard you praise GOD or how many times you show up at church each week. People tend to label themselves as perfect, righteous, or more righteous than others based on what they've done and what they haven't done, but this very act alone is evil in the sight of GOD.

Ephesians 2:8-9: *For by grace are ye saved through faith; and that not of yourselves: it is the gift of God: Not of works, lest any man should boast.*

No man is good; not one. We are but filthy rags, but we are made righteous through CHRIST JESUS, and not from our own works. When we begin to look at the imperfections of others, we lose sight of our own imperfections and we become self-righteous.

Luke 18:10-14: *Two men went up into the*

temple to pray; the one a Pharisee, and the other a publican. The Pharisee stood and prayed thus with himself, God, I thank thee, that I am not as other men are, extortioners, unjust, adulterers, or even as this publican. I fast twice in the week, I give tithes of all that I possess. And the publican, standing afar off, would not lift up so much as his eyes unto heaven, but smote upon his breast, saying, God be merciful to me a sinner. I tell you, this man went down to his house justified rather than the other: for every one that exalteth himself shall be abased; and he that humbleth himself shall be exalted.

The enemy's intent is to come against unity, for unity itself is too powerful a weapon against him. He does this by encouraging us to be imperfect, and then by showing off our imperfections to anyone who's blind enough to see them. He knows that if he could get our eyes off the LORD, and get us to focus on how wrong everyone else is, we would lose our power because we'd no longer walk in love.

Harmony is a beautiful sound to GOD. It is
when HIS people are united as one, despite
their imperfections. Harmony is when two or
more people learn to cover one another in
prayer, sharpen one another with wisdom,
rebuke one another in love, and walk together
as one. Harmony is when two people agree
that no mountain is big enough to separate
them. Their hearts are so focused on doing the
will of GOD that they don't focus on one
another's imperfections. Instead, they correct
and encourage one another. Think about a
choir of men and women singing a song.
Everyone has to sing in harmony for the song
to sound good to those who hear it. What if
one person was to start singing the same song
at a slower pace? They wouldn't be in harmony
anymore, and most of the singers would
become distracted and sing off key. What if
someone stumbled and sang the wrong words?
Most of us have seen this happen before, but

we've also witnessed how a good choir will continue to sing in harmony, despite the error made by one of their members. If they were to stop singing simply because a member made a mistake, the whole song would be a catastrophe.

The same goes for us. Anytime we stop moving together in unity just because we've noticed the imperfections of one of the people walking with us, we stop the entire show.

To GOD, walking in unity is more than just two or more people in agreement; it is two or more people walking in HIS will.

Matthew 18:20: *For where two or three are gathered together in my name, there am I in the midst of them.*

Ecclesiastes 4:12: *And if one prevail against him, two shall withstand him; and a threefold cord is not quickly broken.*

www.ingramcontent.com/pod-product-compliance
Lightning Source LLC
Chambersburg PA
CBHW060241050426
42448CB00009B/1545